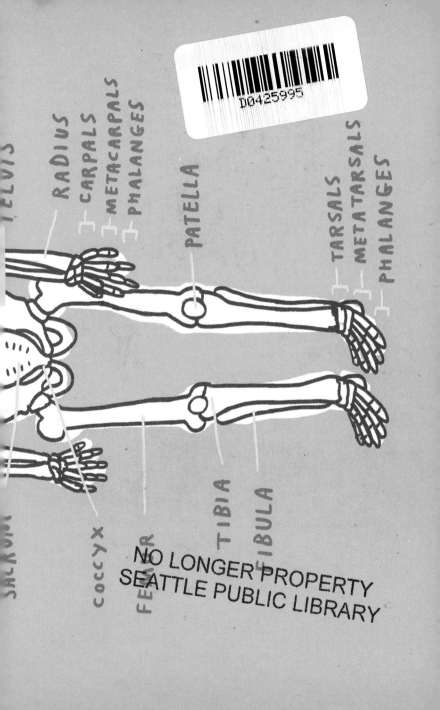

PELVIS

RADIUS

CARPALS

METACARPALS

PHALANGES

PATELLA

TARSALS

METATARSALS

PHALANGES

SACRUM

COCCYX

FEMUR

TIBIA

FIBULA

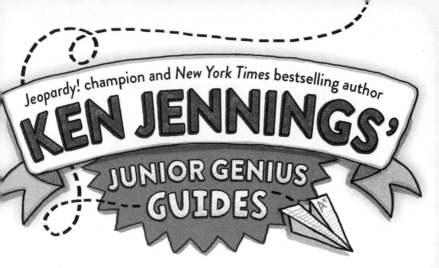

Jeopardy! champion and New York Times bestselling author

KEN JENNINGS'

JUNIOR GENIUS GUIDES

THE HUMAN BODY

BY KEN JENNINGS

ILLUSTRATED BY MIKE LOWERY

SEMPER QUAERENS

LITTLE SIMON

New York London Toronto Sydney New Delhi

THE OFFICIAL
JUNIOR GENIUS CIPHER

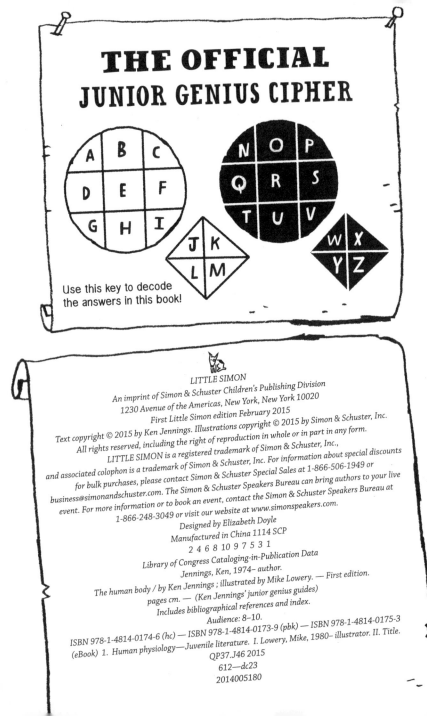

Use this key to decode the answers in this book!

LITTLE SIMON

An imprint of Simon & Schuster Children's Publishing Division
1230 Avenue of the Americas, New York, New York 10020
First Little Simon edition February 2015

Designed by Elizabeth Doyle
Manufactured in China 1114 SCP
2 4 6 8 10 9 7 5 3 1
Library of Congress Cataloging-in-Publication Data
Jennings, Ken, 1974– author.
The human body / by Ken Jennings ; illustrated by Mike Lowery. — First edition.
pages cm. — (Ken Jennings' junior genius guides)
Includes bibliographical references and index.
Audience: 8–10.
ISBN 978-1-4814-0174-6 (hc) — ISBN 978-1-4814-0173-9 (pbk) — ISBN 978-1-4814-0175-3
(eBook) 1. Human physiology—Juvenile literature. I. Lowery, Mike, 1980– illustrator. II. Title.
QP37.J46 2015
612—dc23
2014005180

CONTENTS

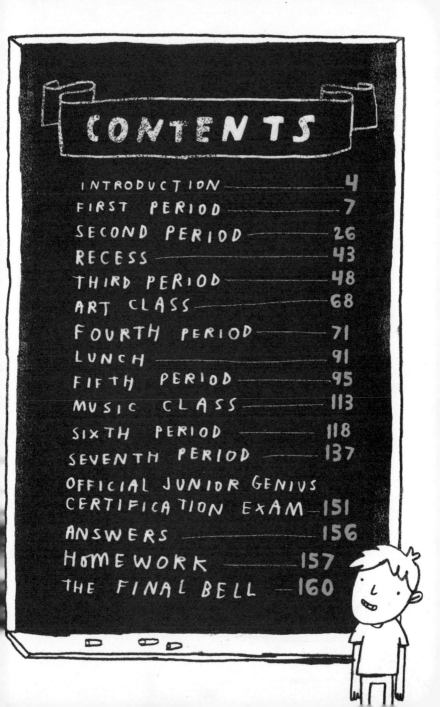

INTRODUCTION

Settle down and find your seats, class. I'm Professor Jennings. But you probably already know that, because I'm such a world-famous authority on absolutely everything. Today we will be studying the most complicated and extraordinary object in the known universe: the human body. I bet most of you know only a tiny fraction of the cool stuff that goes on inside you. Did you all remember to bring your bodies to class today, like I asked? If anyone forgot their body, please raise your hand.

All right! In that case we'll begin in our usual fashion by reciting the Junior Genius Pledge to this picture of Albert Einstein. Please place your right index finger to your right temple and repeat after me.

**With all my fellow Junior Geniuses,
I solemnly pledge to quest after questions,
to angle for answers, to seek out,
and to soak up. I will hunger and thirst for
knowledge my whole life through, and I
dedicate my discoveries to all humankind,
with trivia not for just us but for all.**

If you're afraid you're not quite as smart as Albert Einstein, *don't worry*. You don't have to revolutionize physics to be a Junior Genius. You just need to pay attention to all the amazing things there are to know about the world around you. "*Semper quaerens*" is the Junior Genius motto. That's Latin for "always curious." Even Einstein had to start somewhere!

Are you ready for an in-depth look at your body from the inside? (Not literally—don't worry. That would be dangerous and gross.) Let's begin!

FIRST PERIOD

BEING HUMAN

Junior Geniuses, your body is a wonderland. Nothing personal! I just mean that if you are human, you are an amazing piece of biological machinery. If you are not human, please let me know immediately. We would like to dissect and study you for the upcoming Junior Genius Guides: *Alien Beings*.

The chemicals in your body are nothing special—common stuff you could buy with a little allowance money. In fact, you could recreate most of your body just by turning on a faucet. More than half of you is actually water!

65% OXYGEN

18% CARBON

← 10% HYDROGEN

← 3% NITROGEN

← 1% CALCIUM

← 1% PHOSPHORUS

← 2% OTHER

So, if you are an eighty-pound human looking to rebuild your body with a chemistry set, buying the elements shown in the chart on page 7 would set you back about $160. More than half the money would go to buying potassium, a kind-of-rare mineral found in foods such as oranges and bananas. Your body needs potassium to keep your blood pressure healthy and your muscles working.

EXTRA CREDIT

Your body doesn't need gold to survive, but you do have some in your tissues, from tiny traces of it in the food you eat and water you drink. But you're not going to strike it rich by selling your boogers and earwax to a late-night gold infomercial! The total amount of gold in your body is about the size of a grain of sand.

But when you *combine* the elements in your body, your value skyrockets. Let's say you sold every part of you on the open market—your organs, your bone marrow, your DNA, your antibodies. I would advise against this, however. Not only is it illegal, but you sort of need some of that stuff. But if you had a clearance sale and *everything* had to go, your body could bring in about $45 million!

That's because your body is made of very ordinary elements combined in extraordinary ways.

LADDER PERFECT

Like all other life on earth, human beings are carbon-based. This means that the big, complicated molecules that power us, like proteins and carbohydrates, are all based on the element carbon. Yup, the same stuff that charcoal and diamonds and graphite are made out of. Your body has enough carbon in it to provide the graphite for more than six thousand pencils!

DOUBLE HELIX

One of the most important of these carbon-based molecules is *deoxyribonucleic acid*. Most people call it DNA to save time, and because it's much easier to spell. DNA is a long, skinny molecule shaped like a twisted ladder (or a "double helix," as a biologist would say).

Why is DNA so complicated? Because it contains all the information necessary to make you . . . you. It's how a skin cell knows how to divide itself into new skin cells, and how a liver cell knows how to make new liver cells. There's a reason why dogs don't give birth to kittens and cats don't give birth to

puppies, and that reason is DNA.

GENES

The DNA ladder is divided into long sections called *genes*, which contain instructions on how to pass along heredity information. Do you have brown eyes? Eye color is a gene. Curly hair? The ability to roll your tongue? Morton's Toe? (That's when your second toe is longer than your big toe.) Those traits are all in your genes.

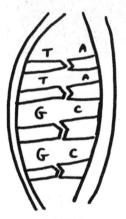

BASES

The rungs of the ladder in each molecule of DNA are chemicals called *bases*. There are four different bases: adenine, guanine, thymine, and cytosine. You know what? Let's keep it simple and call them A, G, T, and C. The pattern of As, Gs, Ts, and Cs on your DNA molecules is like a secret code that contains all the instructions your cells needed to grow into a person. Your whole *genome*—the entire code—is three billion base pairs long. That's enough space to encode an entire shelf of encyclopedias!

MR. GREEN GENES

DNA isn't just a human thing, Junior Geniuses. Pretty much *all* life on earth is based on DNA. Don't get me wrong, I love humans. We are the only organisms on earth with speech, opposable thumbs, video games, *and* pizza. But not everything in our genome is so special. Did you know that . . .

99% of your DNA is the same as a **chimpanzee's**?

97% of your DNA is the same as an **orangutan's**?

80% of your DNA is the same as a **mouse's**?

50% of your DNA is the same as a **banana's**?

You may not be yellow, potassium-rich, and delicious on cereal, but you and bananas are distant branches on the same family tree—the tree of life on earth.

PIECES OF ME

Your DNA is found in every single cell of your body. In fact, there are almost six feet of DNA crammed into each tiny cell. Since the human body has about forty trillion cells in it, that means that you contain more than *forty-five billion miles* of DNA . . . enough to stretch between the sun and Pluto twelve times!

But what is a cell exactly? In 1665 the British scientist Robert Hooke was looking through a microscope at a thin slice of cork. He was surprised to see this:

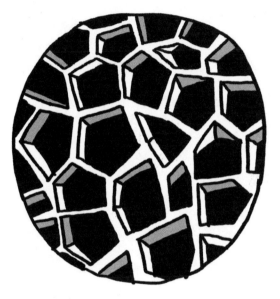

The wood was divided into boxy structures, which reminded him of small rooms. He called them *cells*, like the small rooms where monks or prisoners lived, and the name stuck. Cells are the building blocks of life. All the tissues that make up life on earth, from rose petals to jellyfish tentacles to human brains, are made out of cells.

Human cells aren't boxy like the ones Hooke saw. Only plant cells, it turns out, have rigid walls. Under a very powerful microscope, one of your cells might look more like this.

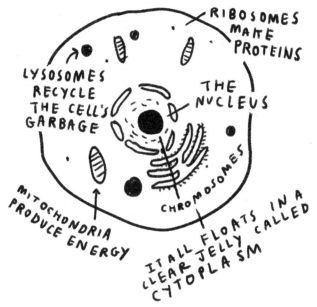

RIBOSOMES MAKE PROTEINS

LYSOSOMES RECYCLE THE CELL'S GARBAGE

THE NUCLEUS

MITOCHONDRIA PRODUCE ENERGY

CHROMOSOMES

IT ALL FLOATS IN A CLEAR JELLY CALLED CYTOPLASM

You have many different types of cells. A bone cell is very different from a brain cell, which is very different from a blood cell. This is a good thing, or you would be a very strange-looking person indeed.

YOUNG AT HEART

Keeping all the cells of your body up-to-date is a never-ending job. Every minute, cell division replaces *ninety-six million* dead cells all over your body. Blink your eyes once. Go ahead. Guess what? During that blink you got half a million new cells! Congratulations!

Are you around ten years old? Maybe a little less, maybe a little more? Here's a secret: so am I, and so are your grandparents, and so is every other adult you know. Because human cells die and get replaced every decade or so, that means that the average age of my cells is about ten years. Most of me isn't old enough to drive!

SMALL WONDER

Your body didn't always have forty trillion cells. At first you had only one!

The path toward human life begins when the largest cell in the human body, a female egg cell, is fertilized by the *smallest* cell in the human body, a male sperm cell. These two are a real odd couple. A sperm cell weighs 175,000 times less than the egg, which is the only human cell so large it

can be seen with the naked eye. For the first half hour of existence, you were just a single fertilized cell, called a *zygote*.

How does that one cell eventually know how to turn into bones and nerves and muscles and all the other kinds of cells the body will need? Because human embryos are made of an amazing kind of cell called a *stem cell*. Stem cells aren't specialized. They haven't decided what they want to be when they grow up. They

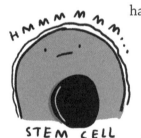

STEM CELL

have the power to turn into a stomach cell or a lung cell or a blood cell or whatever you need. Today scientists are studying ways to use stem cells to save lives by curing diseases or even regrowing whole organs from scratch!

EXTRA CREDIT

For the first five to six weeks of development, you all had something in common. You were female! Well, sort of. It might be more accurate to say that you were all genderless. The Y chromosome, present only in males, doesn't kick in until more than a month after conception. For that first month, growing human embryos of both sexes look exactly the same.

WOMB FOR ONE MORE

About once in every eighty pregnancies, something a little different happens. Either two egg cells get fertilized at once or a fertilized cell splits into two separate embryos.

What happens then? You get twins.

Twins from the same zygote are called *identical twins*. Identical twins have the same genes, which means their DNA is not exactly the same but very, very similar. Even their fingerprints are very, very similar.

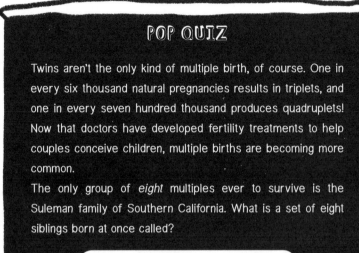

POP QUIZ

Twins aren't the only kind of multiple birth, of course. One in every six thousand natural pregnancies results in triplets, and one in every seven hundred thousand produces quadruplets! Now that doctors have developed fertility treatments to help couples conceive children, multiple births are becoming more common.

The only group of *eight* multiples ever to survive is the Suleman family of Southern California. What is a set of eight siblings born at once called?

Even before they're born, twins have a very special relationship. In ultrasound videos they can be seen reaching for and touching each other in the womb, and they interact socially with each other when they're just a few hours old. As kids, 40 percent of twins even develop a made-up "twin talk" language that they use only with each other!

The unusual closeness between twins can be a life-long thing. For example, let's meet Jim Lewis and Jim Springer. They were adopted as babies and raised by separate families in western Ohio. When they were

finally reunited forty years later, in 1979, they were shocked by the similarities between them. It wasn't just their looks and mannerisms. Both had married women named Linda, and then been remarried to women named Betty. Both had a son named James Allan/Alan and had a dog named Toy. Both drove Chevys, liked woodworking, served as sheriff's deputies, and vacationed at the same Florida beach!

LET'S PUT OUR HEADS TOGETHER

Here's a pair of twins who are even closer: Krista and Tatiana Hogan. They're conjoined twins, meaning the stem cells in their bodies grew together before they were born. Most twins with this condition are joined at the chest or stomach, but the Hogan girls are joined at the brain! When Krista thinks something, Tatiana can hear it. When Tatiana looks at something, Krista can see it too.

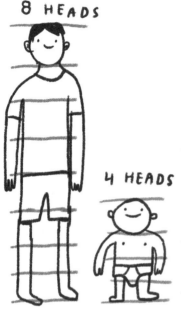

8 HEADS

4 HEADS

I WILL SURVIVE

When you were born, you looked a little different from how you do now. To put it bluntly, you had a big head. An adult's head is about one-eighth of his or her height, but a baby's head is one-quarter of its height! And the baby's head even has a hole in it! When babies are born, the bones of their skull haven't quite grown together yet, so they actually have "soft spots" called *fontanelles* on their heads. Sometimes you can even see it pulsing with their little heartbeat.

EXTRA CREDIT

The human body has 206 bones, but babies are born with about 300! Where do the 94 extra bones go? Do babies lose them like teeth? Nope, the bones just fuse together to form fewer (but bigger) bones as we grow up.

Despite their small size and incomplete bones, babies are tough. Pound for pound a newborn baby is stronger than an ox. In fact, the human body is a pretty resilient piece of equipment. Here are some things your body could possibly survive, if it had to.

NOTE: These are worst-case scenarios, Junior Geniuses. Do not try them at home!

WARNING! WARNING WARNING WARNING WARNING WARNING WARNING WARNING WARNING

Being bitten 173 times by poisonous snakes! Bill Haast, who ran a Florida snake venom lab, handled more than three million poisonous snakes during his career. He made himself immune to snake-bites by injecting himself with deadly venom every day for sixty years, and lived to be one hundred years old.

Being frozen in ice for more than an hour! Anna Bågenholm, a Swedish skier, fell into an icy Norwegian stream in 1999 and couldn't be pulled out for eighty minutes! The extreme hypothermia must have put her body into some kind of hibernation state, because she made an almost full recovery.

WARNING! WARNING

WARNING

WARNING

BOO

DANGER

PO

Cooking steak and eggs... from inside the oven! In 1775 a British scientist named Charles Blagden took his dog, a steak, and some eggs into a room heated to 220°F—hot enough to boil water. After fifteen minutes the steak and eggs had cooked, but Dr. Blagden (and his dog!) were just fine.

An electric drill through the brain! In 2003 a California man named Ron Hunt fell off a ladder onto his drill, which went through his eye and into his brain, and exited out the back of his skull. Hunt never lost consciousness and was rushed to the hospital with the giant drill bit still coming out of his face. Surgeons removed it by unscrewing it like a giant screw!

WARNING

TO THE EXTREME

Despite those amazing survival stories, Junior Geniuses, the human body does have its limits. Let's meet a few of the people who have tested those limits.

Tallest. Robert Wadlow of Illinois had a glandular condition that made his body grow at an amazing speed. By the time he was six years old, he was taller than his father, and his shoe size was 37 AA—a foot and a half long! He was eight-foot-eleven and still growing when he died of an infection in 1940, at age twenty-two.

Shortest. The world's shortest adult on record is a Nepalese villager named Chandra Bahadur Dangi. Dangi has dwarfism and stands just 21.5 inches tall—less than three times the height of this book!

Fastest. At around the seventieth meter of a hundred-meter race, Jamaican sprinter Usain Bolt is traveling at almost twenty-eight miles per hour, the fastest human foot speed ever recorded.

Oldest. Jeanne Calment of Arles, France, lived from 1875 to 1997—more than 122 years! The amazingly healthy Madame Calment took up fencing at age eighty-five and went bicycle-riding until she was one hundred. She is certainly the only person ever to meet Vincent van Gogh (as she did as a girl in 1888) and then go on to record a rap album (which she did in 1996).

Youngest. I hate to brag, my friends, but there was a time when *I* was the youngest person in the world. Not anymore, of course. Now it's a new baby that was just born a second ago. Oh, no, wait. Now it's a different baby. Oops, I'm wrong. Now it's *another* baby. . . .

FOR MEDICINAL PORPOISES ONLY

The world's tallest man in the early 2000s was Bao Xishun, a seven-foot-nine herdsman from northern China. In 2006 a Chinese aquarium asked Bao to come see two sick dolphins that had swallowed shards of plastic. Doctors had been unable to save them, but Bao was able to reach his three-and-a-half-foot arms into the dolphins' stomachs and remove the plastic!

SECOND PERIOD

BRAIN POWER

In 1955 the famous physicist Albert Einstein died in a hospital bed in Princeton, New Jersey. To this day we remember him every time we see a friend do something dumb, and jokingly say, "Nice job, Einstein!" or "Way to go, Einstein!" But the only reason that's funny is because the real Einstein was *not* dumb. Do you get it? We are being sarcastic. The real Einstein was one of the smartest people in history.

EINSTEIN'S BRAIN

THOMAS HARVEY

Thomas Harvey, the doctor who performed the autopsy on Einstein, was curious about the secret of the great man's scientific success. So, without permission from Einstein or his family, he removed the brain, took it home, and had a Philadelphia hospital slice it into 240 cubes! For many years Einstein's brain sat in a cider box under a beer cooler in the Wichita medical lab where Harvey worked.

Finally, in the 1980s, scientists began to study Einstein's brain in detail. They found that some areas of his brain were unusually well-developed for a man his age, while others weren't. But overall the brain wasn't obviously different from most of ours. It wasn't freakishly huge, for example. In fact, it was on the small side.

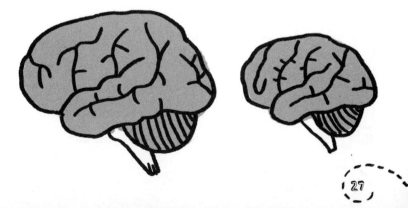

27

The miracle of Einstein's brain is that this 2.7-pound lump of soft, pinkish tissue could totally reimagine the way humankind sees the universe. But when you think about it, Junior Geniuses, we all have the same miracle going on inside our own skulls. You have a lump of soft, pinkish tissue that looks almost the same as Einstein's. And it has the same amazing power to remember facts and memories, feel emotions, solve problems, and come up with ideas.

Back in ancient Greece great philosophers such as Aristotle assumed that people thought with their hearts,

and that the brain was just a big blood-cooling organ. We've learned a lot about the brain since then, but it's so complicated that much of what happens inside our heads remains a mystery. My friends, it's time to explore that mystery. We're going to use our minds to think about . . . our minds! (Did I just blow your mind?)

HEAD HOLE PUN

Today we use "brain surgery" as slang to mean "a really complicated thing." For example:

So it's weird that brain surgery was probably one of the first kinds of medicine that early humans learned to practice! Skulls are often recovered from archaeological digs with big holes in them. That's because people in prehistoric times believed that *trepanning*—the process of making holes in the skull to expose the brain—could cure lots of health problems, from headaches to epilepsy.

Today you've probably noticed that your doctor doesn't drill a hole in your skull every time you have a headache. But many kinds of brain surgery still require a *craniotomy*—temporarily cutting off a flap of bone from your skull with a drill and saw.

That might seem gory, but many patients stay awake through the whole thing! That's right: your brain has billions of nerve cells, but none of them are the kind that can feel pain. Doctors often keep patients awake as they tinker with their brains, so they can ask them questions and find out if the surgery is working or not.

GUITAR HERO

In 2012 a musician named Brad Carter received an electrical device called a pacemaker in his brain to help correct a nerve disorder. Carter played guitar during the entire seven-hour operation! He also streamed photos and videos of the surgery live to the Internet, so fans could watch his playing get stronger and smoother as the pacemaker began to work.

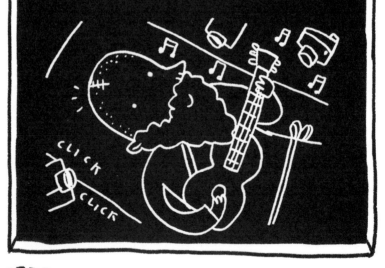

MAKING UP YOUR MIND

This kind of close-up study of the brain has given *neurologists* (doctors who study the brain and nervous system) lots of new information as to how the human computer works.

The surface of your brain—the pink, wrinkly part that you'd see if your doctor were into trepanning—is called the *cerebral cortex*. Those twisty wrinkles and folds are known as *convolutions*, and they help your brain cram more surface area (and more connections, and more thinking) into a smaller space. If you could spread out the surface area of your whole brain, it would be the size of a small tablecloth!

EXTRA CREDIT

Your brain is more than 60 percent fat, making it the fattiest organ in the body. It's amazing that zombies always manage to look so skinny, with their fatty all-brain diet. . . .

Has anyone ever told you that humans use only about 10 percent of our brains? That's just a myth. With new scanning technology, we can see that people really use most of their brains most of the time. Let's take a look.

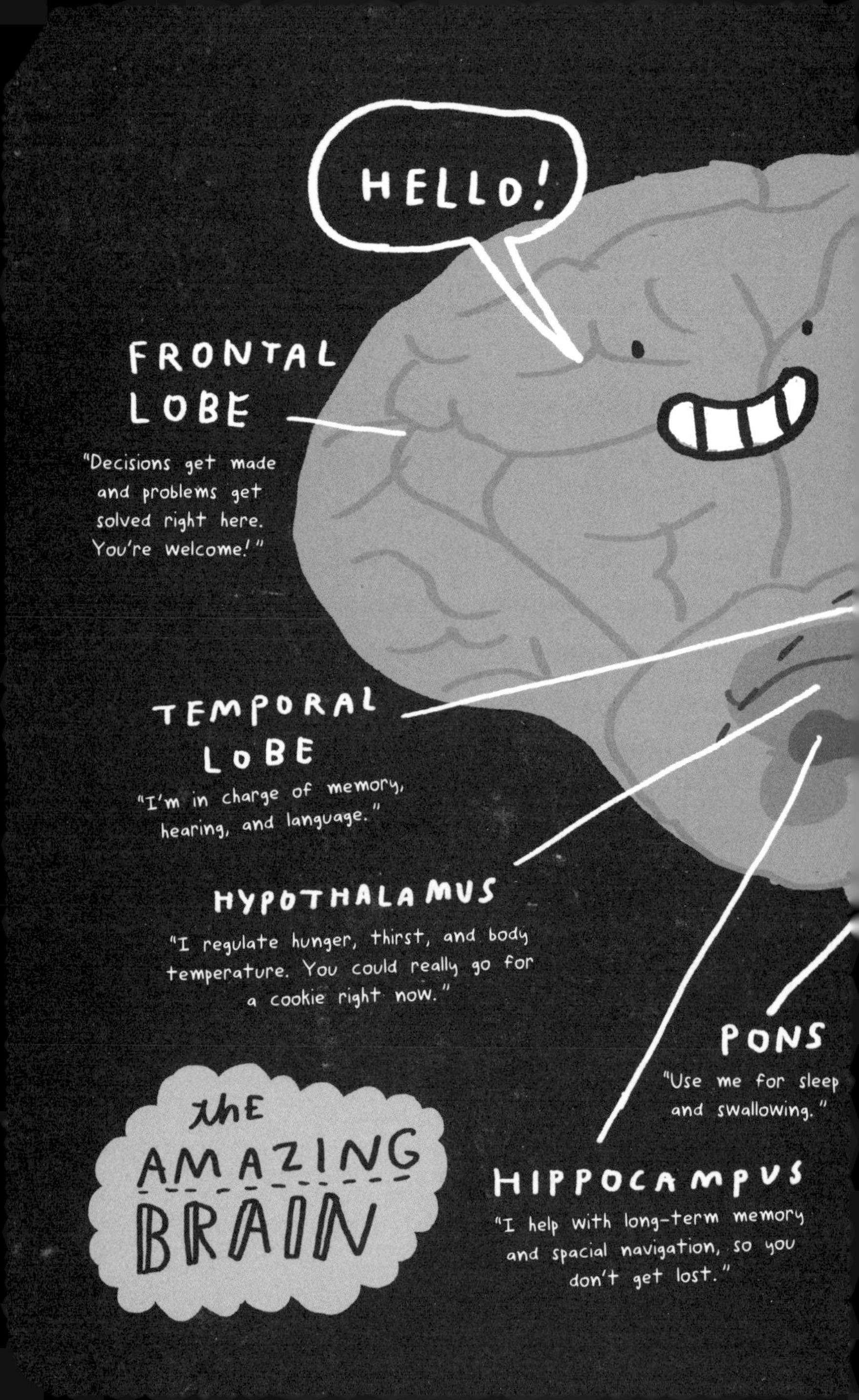
HELLO!
FRONTAL LOBE
"Decisions get made and problems get solved right here. You're welcome!"
TEMPORAL LOBE
"I'm in charge of memory, hearing, and language."
HYPOTHALAMUS
"I regulate hunger, thirst, and body temperature. You could really go for a cookie right now."
PONS
"Use me for sleep and swallowing."
HIPPOCAMPUS
"I help with long-term memory and spacial navigation, so you don't get lost."
the AMAZING BRAIN

PARIETAL LOBE
"I process sensory input coming in from all over your body."

OCCIPITAL LOBE
"Without me you wouldn't know what you were seeing."

CORPUS CALLOSUM
"My more than two hundred million fibers link the two halves (or 'hemispheres') of your brain together."

THALAMUS
"I'm a switchboard, relaying information from touch and pain sensors."

AMYGDALA
"I handle emotional responses like [gulp] fear!"

CEREBELLUM
"I'm in charge of balance and posture. Sit up straight!"

MEDULLA
"I keep your lungs breathing and heart beating. So I'm a pretty big deal."

All these parts work together, but that doesn't mean your brain can really focus on many things at once. True "multitasking" is an illusion. Typically, if you think you're doing several things at once (like finishing your homework while watching TV), what you're really doing is switching rapidly back and forth—and paying less attention to both tasks!

BRAIN MAN

There are exceptions, however. *Savants* are people whose unusually formed brains give them mental superpowers. The movie *Rain Man* is about a savant based on a real-life Utah man named Kim Peek. Peek could read two pages of a book at the same time, one with each eye—even upside down! He was a walking encyclopedia who could remember about 98 percent of everything he ever read. If you told him what day you were born, he could immediately tell you what day of the week that was, and what the newspaper headlines were that day. While reading the phone book, he would mentally add up every seven-digit phone number in each column, getting totals in the trillions! You can see why Kim's friends called him "Kim-puter."

YOU'VE GOT A LOT OF NERVES

Think how amazing the brain is, Junior Geniuses. Even a small child can look at a row of black marks on a white piece of paper, like this one, and immediately decipher that "code" into complicated ideas. How does the lump of fat and protein behind your eyeballs manage to do such difficult jobs?

Well, you have eighty-six billion neurons (nerve cells) in your brain—give or take one or two, of course. Each neuron links to other neurons at connections called *synapses*, little gaps where signals get passed, either by electricity sparking or chemicals squirting. Each neuron in your brain has between one thousand and ten thousand synapses, and all those connections are where the true power of the brain lies. There are so many possible combinations of neural pathways in your head that scientists think the storage capacity of the brain is somewhere around 2.5 petabytes. A *petabyte* is a million gigabytes, so that number in bytes looks like this:

2,500,000,000,000,000

If your brain were a television DVR, that would be enough space to hold three hundred *years'* worth of TV shows. So don't ever tell me your brains are full, Junior Geniuses! There's always room for more amazing information up there. The only challenge is getting interested enough so that you remember it.

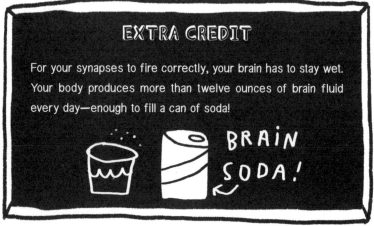

EXTRA CREDIT

For your synapses to fire correctly, your brain has to stay wet. Your body produces more than twelve ounces of brain fluid every day—enough to fill a can of soda!

BRAIN SODA!

A HEAD OF TIME

Your brain processes about four hundred billion actions and reactions every second, so it has to be fast. Your nervous system's fastest signals travel almost two hundred miles per hour. That sounds fast, but it's much slower than electricity in a wire, and there are more than forty-five *miles* of nerves in your body. That time lag means that your brain is always processing things that happened about eighty milliseconds ago. In other words, all people live eighty milliseconds in the past at all times.

Our brain's relationship with time is a funny thing. Have you ever glanced at a clock and thought that the second hand stayed frozen for a weirdly long second before moving on? This is an illusion called *chronostasis*. See, your vision shuts down when your eyes make quick movements, so that the sudden blur of motion doesn't make you dizzy. In fact, you're blind for about forty minutes every day while your brain masks out blinks and quick eye movements! When you look at a clock,  that first second seems extra long because your brain is going back in time to fill in what you missed while your eyes were moving.

In general your brain stretches out time when there's a lot going on. That's why time seems to pass more slowly in childhood than it does in adulthood—because kids are doing so many new things for the first time. If you want to have a longer-seeming life, that's the secret, Junior Geniuses. Keep trying lots of new things, and enjoy each moment!

Babies, on the other hand, have no clue about time. Until you were about a year old, you had no idea that things could exist when you couldn't see them. This is called *object permanence*, and it's why babies love a good game of peekaboo so much. When you hide behind a door, they actually think you're disappearing!

POP QUIZ

One more surprising fact about time and the brain: You can stay conscious for up to twenty seconds after your head gets cut off! During the French Revolution scientists had plenty of chances to study this effect, because lots of people were losing their heads. What is the name of the head-chopping device used for French executions back then?

◣□□ �◗◿◥◥◖◣◤◢□

MIND OVER MATTER

The brain, as you know, is in charge of every other system of your body. That means the health of your brain can have a big impact on whether the rest of you is healthy.

Scientists have found that between 75 and 90 percent of all visits to a doctor can be traced back to a stressed brain.

But this means the brain has amazing powers to heal the rest of you as well. Have you ever heard of the *placebo* ("pluh-SEE-boh") effect? That's when someone is given a fake medicine and told that it will make him or her better. In many cases the useless pill actually works . . . because the patient believes it will!

Doctors have found that the colors of placebo drugs are important: fake white pills work for stomach problems, fake green pills are good for anxiety, and fake yellow pills cure depression. You can get people to act drunk by giving them flavored water and telling them it's alcohol. Some doctors even give patients fake surger-

ies, cutting them open but not fixing anything—and many times these surgeries are just as effective as the real thing.

The placebo effect is not fully understood even today. In some tests doctors have seen placebo pills work even when patients are told beforehand that the pills are fake! But it just goes to show how big an effect your brain can have on your health. Now that you know about the placebo effect, I want you to take three slow sips of water. That's a powerful treatment that will make you love Junior Genius books and buy multiple copies of all of them!

BLAME IT ON THE BRAIN

The brain's amazing power means that when it isn't wired quite right, things can get weird. We've all had *anomia*—"tip of the tongue" syndrome, where you suddenly can't remember a familiar word or name. Here are some very unusual brain disorders with their even more unusual names. (Assuming I can remember them.)

Prosopagnosia. The inability to recognize faces. You can see everyone you know just fine . . . but you can't tell them apart.

Hyperthymesia. The opposite of amnesia. You remember what happened to you on every single day of your life.

Astasia-abasia. You lurch around and dramatically fall over—but only when someone or something is there to catch you.

Clinical lycanthropy. You believe you're an animal. Most people with this syndrome think they're wolves, but others think they're bees, frogs, birds, tigers, and even hyenas.

Micropsia and macropsia. Also known as "Alice in Wonderland syndrome." You think that big things are tiny, or small things are gigantic.

Synesthesia. Your senses get mixed up, so you can see colors of music, taste words, and smell numbers or days of the week. Mmm, Wednesday smells like Triscuits.

HOMEWORK

It's not that hard to fool your brain. Take a look at the the words in this very sentence. Notice anything strange? Look again. Your eyes saw that the word "the" appeared twice. Why didn't your brain?

Sentences that are hard to say are called *tongue twisters*, but really your tongue is working just fine. It's the speech part of your brain that gets twisted by similar sounds. According to the Guinness World Records, the world's toughest tongue twister is:

The sixth sick sheik's sixth sheep's sick.

In 2013 a team of neurologists found that this one is even trickier:

Pad kid poured curd pulled cold.

Can you get your brain to say either one five times fast? Or try annoying some grown-ups with them! Grown-ups love tongue twisters.

There's one more brain disorder you need to be aware of, Junior Geniuses: *sphenopalatine ganglioneuralgia*. That's the fancy medical term for "brain freeze"—you know, that headache you can get from eating ice cream too fast! Doctors recommend curing an ice-cream headache by pressing your tongue firmly against the roof of your mouth.

RECESS

Why do teachers send you outside for a recess a few times during every school day? It's not because they're tired of you and want to gossip with the other teachers. Well, it's not *only* because of that.

Your teachers know that school is mostly *sedentary*, a fancy word meaning "requiring a lot of sitting." Sitting on something may be a nice, relaxing way to spend an afternoon, but it can kill! Scientists have found that about 10 percent of diabetes, heart disease, and cancer can be blamed on physical inactivity.

Can a short break on the soccer field or the monkey bars actually change that? It can! People who exercise for just fifteen minutes a day live, on average, three whole years longer than those who don't. And exercise even makes you smarter. Tests have found that students learn and remember things better right after finishing a fitness routine. So if you want to be a real Junior Genius, you need study breaks.

Your butt may like to sit, but your butt is not the boss of you! Say no to your butt. Here are some ideas to get it into gear for a few minutes.

DR. SIMON SAYS

You've played Simon Says, right? It's a follow-the-leader game where everyone copies what one player does—as long as the leader says "Simon says" before giving the order. If you accidentally follow an order that "Simon didn't say," you are out. But in this version of the game, Simon has been to medical school. Instead of saying "Simon says touch your toes!" he might say "Simon says touch your *hallux*!" (The hallux, you see, is the medical name for your big toe.) Here are some more weird words for body parts you never knew had names. For more ideas, Simon says, "Try an anatomy book."

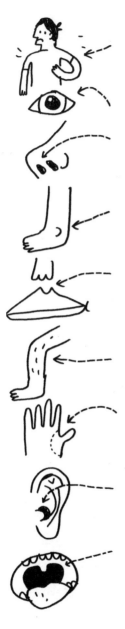

ACNESTIS—the part of your back that you can't scratch

CANTHUS—the corner of the eye

COLUMELLA—the bridge between your nostrils

MALLEOLUS—the bony bump on the side of your ankle

PHILTRUM—the little groove in the middle area of the upper lip, extending to your nose

POPLITEAL FOSSA—the back of the knee

THENAR EMINENCE—that fleshy pad at the base of your thumb

TRAGUS—the small pointed bump of the outer ear

UVULA—that thing dangling in the back of your throat

LUNG HOCKEY

You don't usually notice, but your lungs breathe more than twenty-two thousand times a day. In fact, I bet you're breathing right now! (Until you read those words. Then you stopped. Please start again soon.)

Here's a game to give your lungs a workout. Mark off two goals about six feet wide at opposite ends of your playing space. Place a Ping-Pong ball in the center of the floor and divide up into teams. Each team is trying to score by getting the ball into the opponent's goal—*without touching it*. The only way to move the ball is by blowing on it through a straw. Game is to three goals, or until everyone gets light-headed and passes out.

BRAINSTORM

Everyone looks at the diagram of the brain on pages 32–33 and chooses a part of the brain they want to be. (It's fine—more fun, even—to have multiple players be the same brain part.) Then everyone sits down in a circle of chairs—except for one player who is "It." "It" represents the elusive miracle of human consciousness, and stands in the empty center (or "synapse") of the brain. "It" calls out things like, "Hippocampus and amygdala!" and then those players have to hop up and run to a new seat. "It" tries to grab a vacant seat before they're all full. Sometimes he or she can say "Brainstorm!" and that means *everyone* in the brain needs to swap seats!

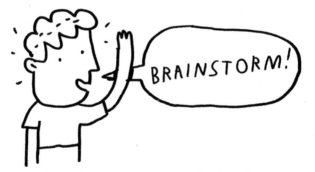

The whole thing is a metaphor for how human consciousness is an epiphenomenon arising holistically from brain activity, and free will is an illusion! Also it's a fun way to kill ten minutes at a party.

THIRD PERIOD

AT YOUR SURFACE

In case you don't have X-ray vision, here is a quick comparison between the outside of the human body and the inside of the human body.

No offense, but you look much better on the outside. Don't get me wrong. All those muscles and organs are a pretty big deal. (Except for the lame ones, like the appendix.) We'll get to them soon. But in this chapter we're going to consider the stuff on the outside of your body: the skin and hair and nails and eyes and earlobes and all that. It's important! If you didn't have all that outside stuff, think how unattractive you would be. Also, you would leak weird fluids everywhere every time you sat down or moved around.

A POUND OF FLESH (OR SIX)

Ask a grown-up what the largest organ in the human body is. Most will probably guess something like the brain or the liver. Nope! The skin is the biggest by far. If an adult's skin were removed, it would weigh six pounds or more, and covers about eighteen square feet—about the size of a picnic blanket.

However, I cannot recommend making a picnic blanket out of human skin. For one thing, your skin cells wear out and get recycled every couple of weeks. That means you shed your skin more often than a snake! You lose six hundred thousand specks of skin every hour, so a good percentage of household dust (the stuff you find under furniture or floating in a shaft of sunlight) is made up of human skin! By the time you turn ten, your entire skin will have been replaced one hundred times.

GOOD-BYE, OLD ME!

EXTRA CREDIT

Troublesome Creek, a tiny town in the hills of eastern Kentucky, has for centuries been home to the Fugate family. The Fugates have a rare genetic condition that makes their skin blue! Their blood cells carry less oxygen than most people's, so their blood is chocolate brown, their lips are purple, and their fingernails are a rich indigo.

SKIN DEEP

You may think that your skin, since it isn't blue, is pretty boring stuff. Junior Geniuses, nothing could be further from the truth!

Here's what your skin looks like up close.

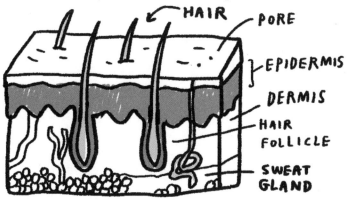

By the numbers, just one square inch of your skin contains:

12 million cells

240 feet of nerves

1,300 nerve endings

650 sweat glands

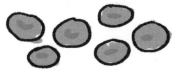
55 feet of blood vessels

One million pores

Why all this equipment? Because the skin does a lot more than just keep you together. Here are some more of its amazing powers:

FEELING! NOTHING MORE THAN FEELING!

All of your skin is wired to sense pressure, heat, cold, pain, texture, and vibration. Your non-hairy skin (like your face and palms) is the most sensitive. Sensitivity may be the reason you have fingerprints as well! Those little ridges make your skin one hundred times better at feeling stuff.

KEEPING YOUR COOL! Your body puts out enough heat every hour to boil half a gallon of water, but your skin always keeps you at a comfy temperature. It does this by dilating (widening) blood vessels and, of course, by sweating! Your feet, for example, can sweat up to a pint a day. But don't blame sweat if your feet stink. Sweat is odorless—it's the bacteria feeding on the sweat that can get smelly.

GLOWING IN THE DARK!

You've seen pictures of *bioluminescent* animals like fish and fireflies, right? Well, your body glows too! You aren't as bright as an anglerfish (no offense), but Japanese scientists have been able to take pictures of people's skin glowing if they use very sensitive cameras.

SCARING YOUR ENEMIES!

Do you get goose bumps on your skin when you're cold or scared? Your body is making its hair stand up on end so you look bigger and scarier—like a frightened cat, or a porcupine with its quills up. (Evolution is slow. Your body hasn't gotten the message that humans are too hairless for this to work very well anymore.)

GRABBING THE SOAP!

Have you ever noticed that your fingers and toes "prune up" when you take a bath? Scientists believe that your skin gets wrinkly so

it can grip things better underwater. Those ridges channel away water like the treads on car tires do.

EXTRA CREDIT

If you don't like your fingers getting wrinkly in the tub, there's a quick fix—cut them off! (Personally, I don't recommend this.) Doctors have noticed that when amputated fingers get reattached, they don't get all raisin-y in water anymore.

HAIR, THERE, AND EVERYWHERE

You may be losing half a million dead skin cells an hour, but in some parts of your body, the dead cells just pile up. In fact, there are so many of them piling up that they get squished into a hard protein called *keratin* and squeezed up out of the skin. Where are these stacks of dead cells? We call them hair and nails!

Yes, from the baldest grandpa to the hairiest uncle, we all have hair growing from our body's millions of tiny hair-producing organs called *follicles*. In fact, humans have as many hair follicles per square inch as chimpanzees do. You have more than one hundred thousand hairs on your scalp alone.

HAIR SUPPLY

Do your parents have to drag you in for a haircut, kicking and screaming? Your hero should be Tran Van Hay, a farmer from the southern tip of Vietnam. Between the 1950s and his death in 2010, Tran never got a haircut. His hair grew to be more than twenty-three feet long and weighed twenty-three pounds! Eventually Tran got so top-heavy that he couldn't even work his farm or take a taxi. He said he washed his hair every six years . . . but let's be honest, shampooing twenty-three feet of hair probably takes about six years!

Is your hair straight, wavy, or curly? This depends on the shape of the hair shaft itself. Round follicles produce round hair shafts, which lie straight. Oval follicles make wavy hair, while flatter follicles make curly hair.

The color of our hair varies depending on how much of a pigment called *melanin* is found in the fiber. Melanin can be brown or black—red hair is caused by a special pinkish type called *pheomelanin*. As we get older, the pigment cells in our follicles die off, and our hair might turn gray or white.

Hair cells may be dead, but they grow very fast. Of all the cells in your body, only bone marrow grows faster than hair. In total you grow about 125 feet of hair every day! Facial hair grows fastest—and it's the strongest, too. Pound for pound, your toughest hair is as strong as copper wire or Kevlar. One head's worth of hair could hoist two elephants into the air!

Hair and nails do *not*, however, keep growing after death. That's just a myth. Once you're in the ground, my friends, it's too late to think about growing out your bangs.

OH, SAY, CAN YOU SEE?

After the brain, the eyes are the most complex organs in the human body. And the thing about the eye being a "window to the soul" isn't just an old proverb. Studies show that your pupils grow by as much as 45 percent when you're looking at someone with whom you're in love.

Like the back of your head, your eyes are one part of your body that you *can't* see without the aid of a mirror. Let me help you take a closer look.

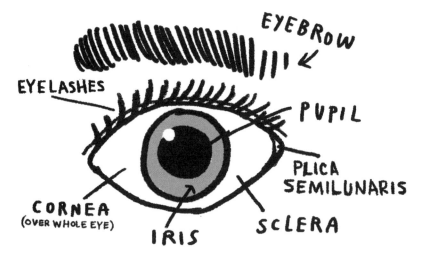

EYEBROWS—Evolved to keep rain and sweat out of our eyes.

CORNEA—The outer layer of your eye has no blood supply, and gets most of its oxygen from the air.

IRIS—The colored part. About one person in every 150 has a rare condition called *heterochromia*—eyes of two different colors!

PUPIL—From the Latin word for "doll," since you see a miniature version of yourself reflected in other people's pupils.

SCLERA—We are the only primates whose eyes have "whites."

TEAR DUCTS—Babies often cry—but without tears! Our lacrimal glands don't start making tears until we're more than a month old.

PLICA SEMILUNARIS—A leftover third eyelid we don't use anymore!

EYELASHES—Protect the eye from debris. The magician Harry Houdini taught himself to pick up pins with his lashes!

WITH ALL YOUR MITE

Check out this ugly-looking little guy. The good news is that in real life it's less than half a millimeter long. The bad news—it's living in your eyelashes right now! This is *Demodex folliculitis*, and he and his buddies are parasites who live in the pores and follicles of human faces, most commonly our eyelashes. Eyelash mites spend their days munching away on skin oil and dead skin cells. At least they're harmless.

OUT OF SIGHT

When we say (on a driver's license, for example) what color our eyes are, we just mean the irises. When someone asks you your eye color, you don't say, "Well, my pupils are black, and my sclera is white, and my tear ducts are sort of pinkish . . ."

MUTANT

Ten thousand years ago driver's licenses didn't exist. But if they had, they wouldn't have needed a box for eye color. Back then everyone on earth had brownish eyes of one kind or another. But then, around the end of the Stone Age, one single person somewhere was born with a weird genetic mutation: blue eyes. That mysterious human is the ancestor of every single blue-eyed person on earth today! If you have blue eyes . . . yes, you are a mutant.

SAY CHEESE!

Ever wonder why your eyes look red in photos? The bright light from the flash is bouncing off the bloody tissue behind your *retina* and reflecting back at the camera. When you see red eyes in photos, you're seeing the inside of your own head! WARNING! If you see someone in a photo with one red eye and one white one, call a doctor. This is usually caused by a kind of tumor called *retinoblastoma*. It's very dangerous in kids and is most often diagnosed when people notice it in flash photos!

Whether they look blue or green or hazel or brown, your irises do more than just look good. They control the width of your pupils. Step into bright sunlight, and your pupil squeezes down to just three millimeters across. Walk into a dark room, and it will dilate to three times that size, to let in more light. Some historians think that this is why pirates wore eye patches. When going belowdecks, they could just switch their patch to the other eye and see normally!

Behind the pupil sits a clear structure called the *lens*, which focuses light across the inside of your eye back onto the sensitive layer of tissue called the *retina*.

As you can see, the retina sees everything upside down! When the optic nerve carries those images to the brain, the brain is—luckily!—good at flipping them right side up again.

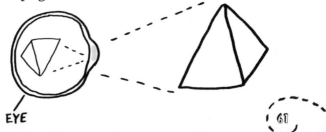

EYE

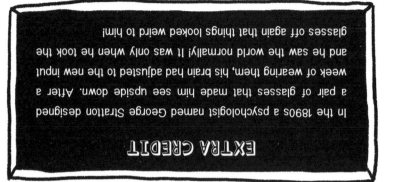

EXTRA CREDIT

In the 1890s a psychologist named George Stratton designed a pair of glasses that made him see upside down. After a week of wearing them, his brain had adjusted to the new input and he saw the world normally! It was only when he took the glasses off again that things looked weird to him!

At the spot where your optic nerve connects to the retina, there are no light-sensitive cells. That means you have a blind spot on your retina!

Here, I can prove it. Take a blank piece of computer paper and lay it down horizontally. Now draw a circle with an *L* on the left size and an *R* on the right side of

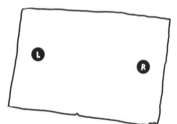

the paper. Then hold the page up about a foot away from your face and close one eye. Focus the other eye on the correct letter (*L* for your left eye, *R* for your right). Now move the page toward or away from your eyes until the other letter disappears. Presto! That's your blind spot.

EYE WON'T GIVE UP

Ninety percent of all our sensory data comes in through our eyes, so the work they do is very important. Here are the five keys to how your eyes are always so good-looking (that is, good at looking at things).

1. THEY ARE SUPERBUFF! The muscles that focus your eyes move one hundred thousand times a day. To flex your leg muscles that much, you'd have to walk fifty miles!

2. THEY HAVE A MUTANT HEALING FACTOR! Your eyes heal as fast or faster than any other part of your body. A scratch on your cornea can be completely repaired within forty-eight hours.

3. NOT ONE BUT TWO TYPES OF CELLS! Your retina has two kinds of receptor cells: cones, which are good at seeing color, and rods, which are good at seeing in dim light. In fact, on a dark night the human eye is capable of seeing a single match being lit fifty miles way! But the

old saying about carrots being good for your night vision? Not true. That was a cover story invented by the British air force during World War II. They didn't want the Germans to know that they had invented airborne radar, so they lied and claimed their pilots' skill was just a result of a carrot-rich diet.

4. SPECIAL BOOGERS! You know that crusty stuff you have in your eyes when you wake up in the morning? It's a special fluid called *rheum* that seals your eyes shut, keeping them from drying out at night.

5. THEY ARE SUPER SPY CAMERAS! A nice digital camera today might take 12-megapixel photos—in other words, photos with twelve million pixels. By comparison the human eye is a 576-megapixel camera! And it never runs out of batteries.

HOMEWORK

You already know if you're left- or right-handed, Junior Geniuses. But did you know that you have a dominant eye as well? That could be important if you ever become a photographer or, um, a professional archer.

Here's how to find your dominant eye. Hold your arms straight out, with your hands held vertically and overlapping, palms facing away from you. Leave a little triangular hole between your hands so you can see a faraway object. *Focus on the object, not your hands.* Now close each of your eyes in turn. Did the object jump sideways out of view when you closed one eye? The eye that you closed is your dominant eye!

Ta-da! You are now ready for the Hunger Games.

LYIN' EYES

Some people—about a third of us—have "normal" vision, or twenty-twenty. That means that at a distance of twenty feet away, you can see what an average person can see from twenty feet away. Twenty-forty is not so good. That means from twenty feet away you can see what the average person sees from forty feet away.

You might need glasses to correct a common vision problem like: **myopia** (nearsightedness)

hyperopia (farsightedness)

astigmatism (blurred vision)

These are all caused by distortion of the lens or cornea.

EXTRA CREDIT

Grown-ups probably warn you about lots of things that are "bad for your eyes": sitting too close to the TV, reading in low light, crossing your eyes, wearing a friend's glasses . . . the list goes on and on. In fact, eye doctors say that *none* of those can damage your vision. You may get a little temporary headache or eyestrain, but that's about it.

Some eye problems are common to everyone. Do you ever see little spots or threads moving slowly over your vision? Good news, Junior Geniuses! You are not crazy. Those are called *floaters*, and everyone sees them. They're just little fibers that float in the *vitreous humor*, the clear jellylike stuff that fills up the inside of your eye.

We often say that optical illusions fool the eye, but optical illusions aren't really your eyes' fault. It's your brain that's confused.

For example, take a look at this.

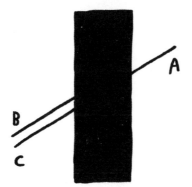

Which of the two lines coming out of the left side of the rectangle are a continuation of A?

It's C. Get a ruler and check. Funny how we trust our eyes, but sometimes they can be dead wrong.

The most serious thing that can go wrong with your eyes is, of course, blindness. But science may be well on its way to curing even that. Doctors are already experimenting with tiny cameras that feed image information directly to the brain via electrical wire. Or we may soon be able to graft new cells directly into the retina. Some scientists use stem cells for this, but others are using 3-D printers to print their own cells! Amazing.

ART CLASS

Thanks to the amazing cone cells in your retinas, Junior Geniuses, you can distinguish a million colors apart. One million! Your eyes can see twenty-five hundred times as many colors as Crayola has ever made.

You might need crayons for today's anatomically correct art project. We're going to give you a quick look inside your own body, with no X-ray machine required. You'll also need:

LARGE PAPER GROCERY BAG

CARDBOARD PAPER TOWEL TUBE

2 DRINKING STRAWS

SCISSORS

3 SMALL CLEAR PLASTIC BAGS

YARN

3333 EMPTY EGG CARTON

SMALLISH BALLOON (RED, IF POSSIBLE)

GLUE

DRY RIGATONI NOODLES

TAPE

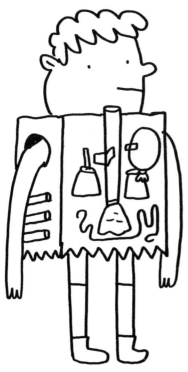

First cut a head hole and two arm holes out of the paper bag. You're going to be wearing the paper bag like a breastplate. But don't put it on yet! It's easier to glue things to paper that you're not inside of.

Start by gluing or taping the cardboard tube vertically in the top center of the bag. This is the *esophagus*, the tube that connects your mouth and stomach. Glue a plastic bag at the bottom of the tube—that's your stomach.

Blow up the balloon a little bit and tie a knot. Tape the balloon just to the right of the esophagus toward the top (so the balloon will be on your left once you're wearing the paper bag). The balloon represents your heart. FOR EXPERTS ONLY: use red and blue crayons on the bag to draw veins and arteries spreading out from the heart.

On the two sides of the esophagus, securely tape the other two plastic bags, as lungs. Tape the two straws in place as *bronchi*, the passages that carry air to your lungs.

Cut the egg cartons into little cardboard cups. Glue a column of them down the center of the back of the bag. These are the *vertebrae*, the bones that protect the spine.

Glue a tangle of yarn below the stomach to represent the *intestines*. Now glue some of your big noodles horizontally to the sides of the bag. Those are the *rib cage*.

Your new inside-out body is done! Carefully put it on. You can blow into the straws to watch your "lungs" inflate, and drop jelly beans down the "esophagus" to see them land in your stomach. But be careful not to wear the bag outside! Your organs are showing.

EEEEK!

FOURTH PERIOD

MOVE THAT BODY

Warning: some of you might find the following illustration *very frightening*. Viewer discretion is advised!

WAS IT SOMETHING I SAID?

This is a skeleton. It's a popular Halloween decoration . . . because it's so scary! Some people probably even find it scarier than other scary Halloween things—ghosts and wolf-men and Draculas.

AHHHHHHHHH

But I've always thought it's a little strange to be scared of the human skeleton, Junior Geniuses. It's like being scared of peanut butter sandwiches when you've just eaten a peanut butter sandwich. I don't want to alarm you, but . . . THERE IS A BIG SCARY SKELETON INSIDE YOU RIGHT NOW!

You should be glad to hear this. Without your bones you would be a shapeless lump of flesh, unable to talk or play mini golf or even hold a pencil. Let's thank our skeletons by learning a little bit about what they are and how they move.

JUNIOR GENIUS JOVIALITY!

Q: Why don't skeletons fight?
A: They don't have any guts.

GENERATION X

If you want to see your skeleton, the best option used to be vultures. Hungry vultures can strip a corpse down to bare bone in just five hours! Nice job, vultures. That is some quick work there.

But now there's an even faster—and less gruesome—way to see what your skeleton looks like. In 1895 a German scientist named Wilhelm Roentgen accidentally discovered a new kind of radiation that could pass through cardboard. He didn't know what these new unknown rays were, so he called them *X-rays*. As one of his first experiments, he put his wife's hand on a photographic plate and exposed it to X-rays. The resulting picture was a bony skeleton hand wearing a

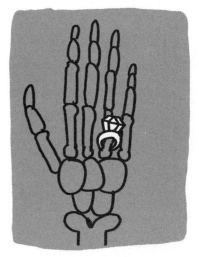

ring. "I have seen my death!" said his shocked wife. But instead, X-rays brought life: countless people have been saved by *radiology*, Roentgen's new science for imaging the inside of the human body.

EXTRA CREDIT

Medical students who spend a lot of time studying the human skeleton often cut Doritos out of their diet. Why? Because of the smell! When students saw through skulls and limbs, they find that human bone dust smells weirdly like corn chips.

BONE APPÉTIT!

Only 15 percent of your body weight comes from bones. This is partly because your bones have spaces inside them. (The insides are filled with a gunk called *marrow*, which is where blood cells are made.) But despite their surprisingly light weight, bones are incredibly strong—stronger than steel, for their weight. A bone the size of a matchbox could hold up nine tons of weight, which is four times what the same size of concrete could support.

What makes bones strong? Minerals! Two-thirds of human bone are made up of crystals of calcium, the same element you find in rocks such as limestone and chalk. The other third is mostly a protein called *collagen*. If you soak a bone in acid, the minerals will dissolve and leave only the collagen. The bone will be so soft that you can literally tie it into a knot.

Calcium in bones is why grown-ups are always after you to drink your milk. At your age your skeleton is still growing every day, and more than 85 percent of girls and 64 percent of boys ages 12 to 19 don't get enough calcium in their diet. You probably need about thirteen hundred milligrams of calcium a day, which is a lot. That's:

4 GLASSES OF MILK

OR

4 SLICES OF CHEESE

OR

6 YOGURTS

OR

x4

4 BUNCHES OF SPINACH

OR

x5

5 HEADS OF BROCCOLI

So remember your dairy, my friends. (Or, if dairy is not a possibility for you, *lots* of leafy green vegetables. Mmm, broccoli.)

EXTRA CREDIT

Broken bones are on the rise in kids nationwide, and calcium deficiency may be part of the problem. But no matter how many trees you fall out of, or how much milk you leave undrunk at lunch, you will probably never beat the record of Evel Knievel, who broke more than 433 bones during his lifetime! Knievel's many health problems had nothing to do with bone density or yogurt. He was a professional daredevil who spent his life crashing his motorcycle into things. Good thing he always wore a helmet!

SKELETON CREW

You have 206 bones in your entire skeleton, from the tip of your skull down to the soles of your metatarsals (your feet). You need them all, but here are a few especially interesting ones:

The cranial and facial bones.

Your skull is actually made up of two sections, the cranium and the face . . . not one bone but twenty-two different ones, most of which meet at immovable joints called *sutures*. In the nineteenth century many scholars believed that you could tell everything about a person by feeling the bumps on his or her skull. This goofy "science" was called *phrenology*, but today, of course, it's been completely debunked.

The clavicle. Also known as the "collarbone," on each side of your body this connects your shoulder blade to the breastbone. The clavicle is one of the most commonly broken bones in the human body.

The hyoid. This horseshoe-shaped guy in the front of your neck helps you swallow. Weirdly, it's the only bone in your skeleton that's not attached to any other bones!

The ribs. Contrary to popular belief, men and women have the same number of ribs: twelve pairs each.

The ossicles. These tiny bones in your ear pass sound along from your eardrum by vibrating. They're called

the *hammer*, the *anvil*, and the *stirrup* because of their shapes. The stirrup, just three millimeters across, is the smallest bone in the body.

The femur. On the other hand, the  femur, inside your thigh, is your longest bone.

The tarsals, metatarsals, and phalanges. One-quarter of all the bones in your body are found in your feet!

HOMEWORK

Your skeleton is weirdly symmetrical. Stick your arms out at your sides and measure your full arm span, from tip of middle finger to tip of middle finger. Compare that distance to your height. In most people it's almost exactly identical!

ROCKING THE JOINT

If you measure your height in the morning and then again at night before bed, you'll be surprised to find that you're shrinking! That's right, people are generally about an inch taller in the morning. Spending all day walking around with earth's gravity pushing down on you tends to squish your skeleton, by curving your spine and compressing your joints slightly.

Joints are the places where bones meet, and they allow our skeleton to move. There are lots of different kinds.

For Example: **Not Unlike:**

Ball-and-socket joints — YOUR SHOULDER — A COMPUTER JOYSTICK

Hinge joints — YOUR ELBOW — A DOOR HINGE

Pivot joints — YOUR NECK — AN OFFICE SWIVEL CHAIR

The space between bones at a joint is filled with a liquid called *synovial fluid*, which helps the bones slide around nicely. If you want to hear your synovial fluid at work, try cracking your knuckles. The sound you hear is caused by bubbles forming inside the joint when it gets extended—and then quickly popping.

Mom or Dad might be annoyed by the noise, but you can tell them that, according to several studies, cracking your knuckles isn't bad for you. The best experiment was reported in 2009 by a man named Donald Unger, who spent more than fifty years cracking the joints on his left hand but never on his right hand. He never developed arthritis in either hand.

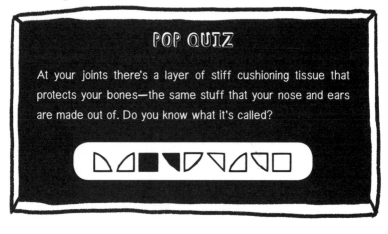

POP QUIZ

At your joints there's a layer of stiff cushioning tissue that protects your bones—the same stuff that your nose and ears are made out of. Do you know what it's called?

MUSCLE-BOUND

If all you had under your skin was a skeleton, then all you could do was stand there, like the skeletons in a medical college or a Halloween store. You would probably get bored, unless there was a TV nearby. Luckily, we all have something that lets us *move* our bones. We have muscles!

There are about 650 skeletal muscles attached to your bones, making up 40 percent of your body weight. That may seem like a lot, but don't get too cocky, Junior Geniuses. The tiniest caterpillar has many more.

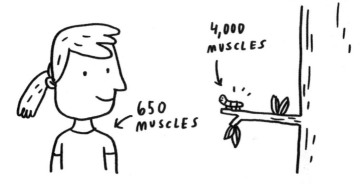

Muscles are attached to bones by tight little ropy things called *tendons*. Want to feel a tendon? The springy stuff connecting your calf to the back of your heel is the Achilles tendon, named for the warrior in Greek mythology who had his only weak spot there.

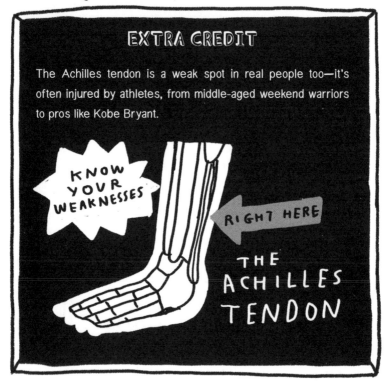

You can also see your tendons show by tightening the muscles in your arm or neck. Those gross strands that appear on the inside of your elbow and in your throat when you flex? Tendons.

Ligaments are similar to tendons, but they connect bones to bones, usually to stabilize important joints. In 2013 doctors in Belgium actually discovered a *new* knee ligament. This little guy, which the doctors called the *anterolateral ligament*, had been sitting in our knees all along, but it's so thin and easy to miss that it had never appeared in medical textbooks!

MOTION PLUS

Muscles go to work when your brain sends them electrical signals, telling them to contract. Muscles are made of thin filaments that can slide past each other, sort of like when you pull in a rope hand over hand. This process shortens the muscle, and the muscle contracts.

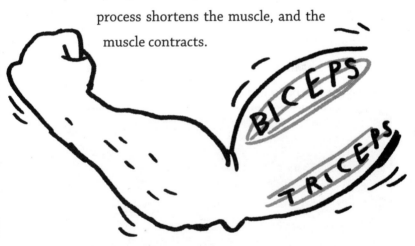

Let's experiment with the muscles in our upper arm. The muscle on the inside of your arm, like all your muscles, has a fancy Latin name. It's your *biceps brachii*. When you contract your biceps, your arm bends. Try it once! If you are now tired, please consider some time at the gym. It's never too early to make good fitness choices.

But here's the problem: the only thing your biceps can do is pull. If all you had in your upper arm were the biceps muscle, your arm would now be bent forever, like a mannequin's. You would have only one bend per arm per lifetime. Use it well! But luckily, muscles come in pairs. On the outside of your upper arm is another muscle called the *triceps*. When that muscle contracts, your arm straightens.

Every muscle in your body is important. Just taking a single step requires moving two hundred muscles in perfect coordination. No wonder it takes babies a year or so to get the hang of it.

EXTRA CREDIT

Believe it or not, there are a few parts of the body that have no muscles at all. In fact, there are ten—your fingers! The muscles that bend your fingers and thumbs are all found in your palms and forearms. Only the tendons of these muscles go all the way into the fingers.

PUMPED UP

What's the strongest muscle in your body? Some say it's the tongue, but there's no science to back that up. (Also, the tongue is made up of eight muscles rather than just one. But it is unique in the human body in that it's only attached on one end!) Here are some better candidates for the bodybuilding title.

Your jaw. Because it's so short, the *masseter* muscle in your jaw can bite down with incredible strength—975 pounds of force in some cases.

Your butt. All muscle fibers have about the same strength, so your larger muscles are, in a way, the strongest ones in total. And the largest muscle in the body is the *gluteus maximus* in each of your buttocks. You need it to run, jump, and climb. Butts aren't just for sitting, my friends!

Your calf. No muscle pulls with greater force than the *soleus*, in your lower leg. Without it you couldn't walk or even stand up straight. The average person walks far enough in their life to circle the earth three times, so the soleus has to be tough.

Your eye. As we've seen, no muscles are stronger for their size than the ones that move your eyes. And no wonder—an hour of reading requires nearly ten thousand muscle movements.

Your uterus. Granted, some of you may not have a uterus. You are missing out! This amazing organ of a woman's body, where babies develop, is lined with a layer of muscle called the *myometrium*. When it's time for the baby to be born, this muscle can squeeze with incredibly strong contractions.

WIMPY, WIMPY, WIMPY

As a contender for weakest muscle, how about the *psoas minor*? Located between your spine and your pelvis, the psoas minor is hidden by its larger cousin the *psoas major*. In fact, the psoas minor is so unimportant that half of all people don't even have it!

THE TORTOISE AND THE HARE

There are actually two kinds of fibers in your skeletal muscles.

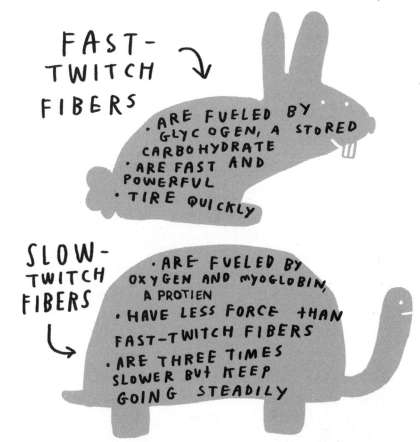

FAST-TWITCH FIBERS

- ARE FUELED BY GLYCOGEN, A STORED CARBOHYDRATE
- ARE FAST AND POWERFUL
- TIRE QUICKLY

SLOW-TWITCH FIBERS

- ARE FUELED BY OXYGEN AND MYOGLOBIN, A PROTIEN
- HAVE LESS FORCE THAN FAST-TWITCH FIBERS
- ARE THREE TIMES SLOWER BUT KEEP GOING STEADILY

When I was your age, I would look at anatomical drawings and think, "Well, I see bones and muscles and organs and fat, but where's the meat? Don't people have meat?" Well, if you eat meat, the animal tissue you're eating is mostly muscle. Muscle *is* meat.

And you know how at Thanksgiving the turkey has white meat and dark meat? The white meat in the breast is slow-twitch tissue, and not built for endurance. (Turkeys don't fly much, so these muscles rarely get used.) The dark meat, in the legs and thighs, is colored by reddish myoglobin, which delivers oxygen to those fast-twitch muscles.

PEOPLE FOOD

If meat is muscle, what would we taste like to a hungry bear or lion? Junior Geniuses, unlike many other children's books authors, *I do not endorse cannibalism.* But the simple fact is that sometimes people eat other people. This might be for ritual reasons (certain South Pacific tribes) or survival or criminal ones (um, use your imagination).

In 1931 an American journalist named William Buehler Seabrook spent eight months with the Gueré cannibals of West Africa. In his book *Jungle Ways* he reported that human meat smelled like beef when cooked, but was lighter in color. It tasted "like good, fully developed veal."

Our mix of muscle fibers explains why people can run both sprints (fast-twitch!) and marathons (slow-twitch). Lots of species, from cheetahs to deer to ostriches, can run faster than people, but we are much harder to beat over long distances. Because our ancestors survived by

tracking speedy prey like antelopes, humans are better at endurance running than almost any other animal. Over

marathon distances, trained runners have even beaten horses. Thanks, slow-twitch muscle!

SMOOTH TALK

Running a marathon and kicking a soccer ball are definitely important things we couldn't do without muscles. But the skeletal muscles we use to move are just one kind of muscle tissue.

What about all the *involuntary* moving your body needs to do? You don't have to think about it every time you need to push food from your esophagus into your stomach, or dilate an artery to change your blood pressure. These parts of your body are lined with a kind of muscle called *smooth muscle*, because its fibers don't come in big stripy bundles like your skeletal muscles do.

In general it's good that you don't need to concentrate on contracting blood vessels or intestinal walls. But involuntary muscles can have their downside. You have a muscle called the *diaphragm* that helps you breathe air into your lungs. Which is great—until something short-circuits and the diaphragm starts contracting suddenly when it's not supposed to. That's when you get . . . the hiccups.

You actually have a third kind of muscle as well—involuntary like smooth muscle but as powerful as skeletal muscle. It's called *cardiac muscle*, and it's what your heart is made of. We'll be taking a closer look at that a little later on. Now, I hope all that talk about cannibalism made you hungry, because it's time for lunch.

DIAPHRAGM

LUNCH

Thank goodness we live in the twenty-first century, Junior Geniuses. Obviously our time isn't perfect. We face serious problems like climate change, traffic jams, and reality TV. But at least we have modern medicine to keep us from dying in lots of painful ways! In the year 1900 the average American lived to be only forty-seven years old. In fact, two-thirds of all retirement-age people (sixty-five and up) who have *ever* lived on earth are alive right now.

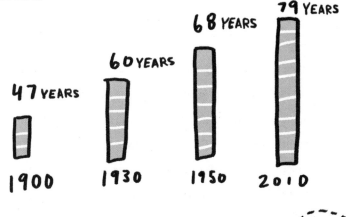

47 YEARS — 1900
60 YEARS — 1930
68 YEARS — 1950
79 YEARS — 2010

In the nineteenth century the only treatment for lots of infections and injuries was amputation. Uh-oh, your skinned knee got infected? Better cut off your leg! Most of the surgeries done during the Civil War—more than fifty thousand of them!—were amputations.

Surgeons at the time believed that the most important part of a safe amputation was speed. (Remember, modern anesthesia hadn't been invented either, so patients *definitely* preferred speed too.) Dr. Robert Liston, a Scottish physician, was the most famous speed surgeon of his day. He could take off a whole limb—muscle, bone, and all—in just twenty-eight seconds!

I'm happy to report that today, with modern antibiotics, amputated limbs are much less common. So uncommon, in fact, that it's cool to experience them in sandwich form! Here's a little anytime snack that you can make all by yourself and is totally gross. (I mean delicious.)

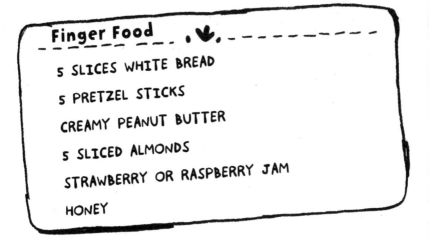

Finger Food

5 SLICES WHITE BREAD

5 PRETZEL STICKS

CREAMY PEANUT BUTTER

5 SLICED ALMONDS

STRAWBERRY OR RASPBERRY JAM

HONEY

Directions

1. Remove the crusts from the bread slices and gently use a rolling pin to squish all the bread slices flat.

2. Place a pretzel stick on each slice of bread and trim the slice so it's the same length as the pretzel. (The pretzel is going to be the "bone" inside each finger.)

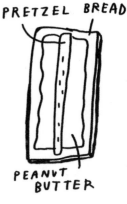

PRETZEL BREAD

PEANUT BUTTER

3. Spread each slice of bread with a thin layer of peanut butter.

4. Now roll each bread slice into a cylinder around the pretzel stick. Make each one more finger-shaped by cutting a few grooves at the "knuckles." Careful with the knife! We don't want any real amputations.

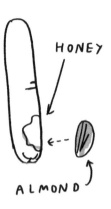

HONEY

ALMOND

5. Round off one end of each "finger" by trimming away diagonal corners and squishing the end into shape. Use a dab of honey to place an almond sliver "fingernail" at the end of each roll.

6. Add a glop of strawberry jam for blood at the other end of each finger. Yuck.

7. Spread all five fingers out on a plate, and enjoy! This is one time when you won't get in trouble for biting your nails.

STRAWBERRY
JAM

FIFTH PERIOD

GROSS ANATOMY

When you were just a fertilized egg inside your mother, which part of you formed first? Of course you don't remember. You were just a lump of cells, without even a phone to take selfies with. So let me remind you.

CLICK

CELL-FIE

Human beings, like many other animals, are *deuterostomes*. This means that we develop out of an opening called a *blastopore*, which becomes one end of our digestive tract. In *protostomes*, such as earthworms and squids, this hole becomes the mouth. But in humans and other deuterostomes, this opening becomes, well, the other end. The anus. DON'T GIGGLE, JUNIOR GENIUSES! THIS IS SERIOUS SCIENCE.

In other words, your whole body started as the hole in your bottom, and grew from there. But this makes perfect sense! Our digestive system—a big tube with food entering one end and leaving the other—is one of the most basic and important things about our bodies. Almost all animals have a "food tube," though the digestive system in an ostrich or an oyster might look very different from yours. Let's learn how yours works. Unlike you did as an embryo, we're going to start with the top end of the tube—the mouth.

CHEWS TO SUCCEED

Don't be too grossed out by this, but by the time a bite of sandwich gets to your stomach, it's already been partly digested—in your mouth! You can thank the dynamic duo of teeth and saliva.

TEETH!

Specialty: Physically breaking food into smaller pieces.

Powers: Covered with enamel, by far the hardest substance in your body.

Weaknesses: The crowns of your teeth are your only body part that can't heal itself. Remember to brush and floss, because the total bacteria count in your mouth is roughly the same as the human population of earth—seven billion!

SALIVA!

Specialty: Contains an enzyme that digests starch.

Powers: Allows you to taste your food, since taste buds work only on liquids. Also contains *opiorphin*, a painkiller stronger than morphine!

Weaknesses: Can make you drool. The salivary glands in your mouth will produce around ten thousand gallons of saliva in your lifetime—a whole swimming pool full of spit!

PLAQUE TO THE FUTURE

Prehistoric humans never flossed, but they had healthier teeth and gums than we do today, since they ate mostly meat, vegetables, and nuts. But as soon as they started to eat sugars and starches, the problems started. Here are the all-time worst time periods in the history of dental care.

50 BC: Ancient Romans use urine as toothpaste.

AD 1000: Vikings file their teeth into sharp points to scare their enemies.

AD 1600: Englishwomen black out their teeth with makeup to look wealthy. (Sugar was very expensive back then.)

AD 1800: The poor would often sell their teeth to make dentures for the rich.

AD 1870: People would have all their teeth pulled as a twenty-first birthday present, and get false ones.

A LICK OF SENSE

Can you tell what this is?

A coral reef? An alien planet? Nope. That's your tongue up close.

You wouldn't be able to taste things—or talk, swallow, or "blow a raspberry" at someone—without your tongue. Those bumps are called *papillae* and give your tongue its rough texture. In fact, the bumps on your tongue give it a distinctive "tongue-print," just as unique to you as your fingerprints. *So if you plan to commit any crimes, please don't lick anything!*

You may have seen a tongue diagram that looks like this.

But a true Junior Genius knows that this kind of "map" is mistaken. First, there are *five* kinds of tastes. The fifth kind of taste is called *savory*, or *umami*, and is found in foods such as beef, potatoes, seafood, and mushrooms.

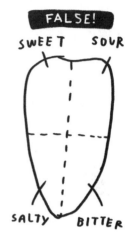

Second, there are no divisions like this on your tongue! Taste buds that detect all five kinds of tastes are found on all parts of the tongue, not to mention the roof of your mouth and the inside of your cheeks and lips.

EXTRA CREDIT

John Harrison, the official taste-tester for Edy's and Dreyer's ice cream, has such a valuable sense of taste that the company has insured his tongue for one million dollars!

Speaking of the lips, I'd like to take a minute to solve two easy lip mysteries.

TWO EASY LIP MYSTERIES, SOLVED

1. "WHY ARE MY LIPS RED?" Lip skin is thinner than your other skin, so the reddish blood vessels show through.

2. "WHY DO MY LIPS GET CHAPPED?" Lips don't have sweat glands or oil-producing hair follicles, so they dry out more easily than other skin.

Wow, those were indeed pretty easy. If you have any other questions about lips, please let me know.

THE ACID TEST

Once food is swallowed, it travels down the esophagus into the stomach. This journey takes about nine seconds—and doesn't rely on gravity, as you might think. Instead your digestive tract has a rhythmic process called *peristalsis* that

pushes food downward in waves. (Imagine someone squeezing toothpaste toward the top of the tube. Sort of like that.) Thanks to peristalsis, it's possible to drink a glass of water while standing on your head. The liquid will still get swallowed "up" into your tummy.

WARNING!

Get a towel before you try this at home! Peristalsis works, but sometimes it leaks.

The stomach is a hollow organ that can hold about thirty-two ounces. (You will eat fifty tons of food and will drink eleven thousand gallons of liquids during your lifetime, but—luckily—not all at once.) For many years thirty-two ounces was exactly *half* the size of a 7-Eleven Double Gulp. In

DOUBLE GULP

STOMACH

2012, 7-Eleven reduced the size of the Double Gulp— but not because it was too big for your stomach, oh no. Because *it was too big for the cup holders in most cars*!

In your stomach the *bolus* from your mouth gets broken down into *chyme*. (These are both words that

doctors made up so they don't have to say "gross chewed-up food" all the time.) Your stomach does this by secreting hydrochloric acid, the same acid that we use to make leather or strip rust off metal. That's right—the acid in your stomach can dissolve razor blades.

How does your stomach stand up to acid that would burn a hole in skin? First, your stomach is coated in a layer of thick mucus. Second, the cells in your stomach lining replace one another very fast—you get a whole new stomach lining once or twice a week. If not for that, your stomach would quickly digest itself!

EXTRA CREDIT

Even stomach acid has its limits. In the 1970s a Dutch woman named Margaret Daalman complained to her doctor about a stomachache. X-rays revealed that her stomach contained seventy-eight spoons and forks! "She seems to have been suffering from some sort of obsession, and every time she sat down for a meal, she would ignore the food and eat the cutlery," her doctor explained.

When your stomach doesn't have any food (or spoons or forks) in it, it will let you know, with classic quotes like:

Borborygmus is the technical term for stomach-rumbling. What you are hearing is peristalsis—your stomach trying to squeeze food downward—only there's nothing left to squeeze. Without any food to muffle these vibrations, they reverberate in your empty stomach just like your voice echoes in a big empty room.

THE HOLE TRUTH

Lots of what we know about digestion comes from the work of a U.S. Army surgeon named William Beaumont. In 1822 Beaumont operated on Alexis Saint Martin, a young Canadian fur trader who had been shot in the side. The wound left a hole right into Saint Martin's stomach, and Beaumont spent the next decade experimenting on the poor guy. He would tie pieces of food to strings, dunk them into Saint Martin's stomach window, and observe the results!

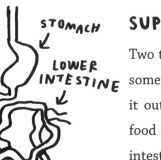

STOMACH

LOWER INTESTINE

SUPER BOWEL

Two to three hours after you eat something, peristalsis squeezes it out of your stomach and the food moves down into the small intestine, where 95 percent of all nutrients are absorbed. That's right, the stomach gets all the hype, but the small intestine is where the real digestive action is.

It's divided into three sections.

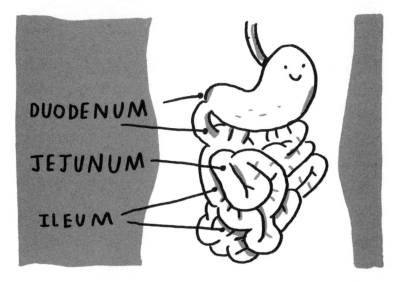

DUODENUM

JEJUNUM

ILEUM

The whole thing is lined with fingerlike projections called *villi* (these are supersmall) and *microvilli* (these are super-duper-small) that increase the surface area of the intestine and help it absorb more food nutrients. If you could spread out that whole surface flat, you'd find that your small intestine has about the same surface area as a tennis court!

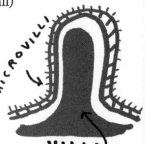

MICROVILLI

VILLI

EXTRA CREDIT

You know that weird queasy sensation you get when a roller coaster goes downhill? That's because, without the effects of gravity, your stomach and small intestine float freely inside you, instead of sitting down nicely like they're supposed to. Astronauts have to get used to that feeling *all the time*!

A HELPING GLAND

The stomach and intestine are surrounded by a bunch of other organs that help out with the digestion process. Let's meet the gang!

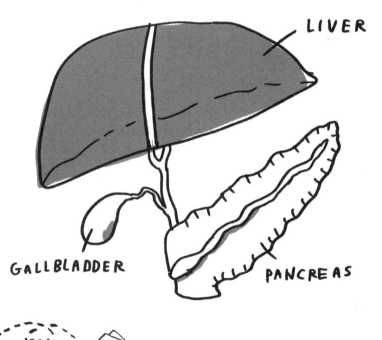

LIVER

GALLBLADDER

PANCREAS

The liver produces *bile*, a fluid that helps your small intestine digest fat and vitamins. (You may have seen bile before, though you probably didn't want to. It's the bitter, yellow stuff that comes up when you barf on an empty stomach.)

But the liver isn't just a digestion sidekick. Of all your internal organs, the liver is a real heavy lifter. (And just plain heavy, period. At 3.5 pounds on average, it's the human body's heaviest internal organ.) Scientists have listed more than five hundred things the liver does for your body, from producing proteins to breaking down toxins.

It's also the only human internal organ that can regenerate itself. You can remove 75 percent of your liver, and the rest will grow back!

The gallbladder stores the bile your liver produces. Sometimes the bile can clump together into big hard lumps called *gallstones*—which can even get as big as a golf ball! In serious cases, surgeons treat this problem by removing the whole gallbladder—you can live just fine without it.

The pancreas is like two organs in one. It's a digestive organ that produces enzymes your intestines need to digest nutrients. But it's also an *endocrine gland*.

The endocrine glands are a separate body system that secretes messenger chemicals called *hormones* into your blood. Your pancreas produces an important hormone called *insulin*, which controls your body's supply of blood sugar.

EXTRA CREDIT!

Some other endocrine glands include the pituitary gland in your brain, the thyroid in your neck, and the adrenal glands above your kidneys. The adrenal glands produce *adrenaline*, a hormone that helps your body act quickly in stressful "fight-or-flight" situations.

Sometimes stressful situations lead to an amazing syndrome called *hysterical strength*. In 1982 a Georgia mother lifted a thirty-five-hundred-pound Chevy Impala four inches into the air, to save her son who was trapped beneath it. And in 2006 a woman in Quebec wrestled a polar bear to the ground to protect two children playing hockey nearby. Doctors aren't sure how these feats are possible. (This kind of thing is hard to test in the laboratory without actually dropping a car or a polar bear onto someone's kids.) But a burst of adrenaline is probably involved.

TAKE THE SHORT GUT

After a few hours in the small intestine, what's left of your dinner oozes into the large intestine—specifically, a part called the *colon*, where water and minerals are absorbed for the next few hours or even days. The food is in no hurry. It knows where it's going next.

The large intestine, confusingly, is only five feet long—much shorter than the "small" intestine, which is more than twenty-two feet long! Its name comes from its diameter—the large intestine is a slightly wider tube than the small one.

Your large intestine is also "large" in population. It's home to more than one hundred trillion bacteria—ten times the number of cells in your body! Luckily, these are "good" bacteria that help keep your intestine healthy and even produce vitamins. But, boy, are there a lot of them! You have about five pounds of creepy-crawlies in your large intestine, enough to fill a large soup can. About half of the dry weight of human poop is dead bacteria.

EXTRA CREDIT

Some of the byproducts of digestion in your colon aren't solids or liquids but gases. Those gas bubbles have to go somewhere—and that's why you pass intestinal gas (or *flatulence*, as a doctor would say) an average of fourteen times a day! (Come on, admit it, that was you.) Most of the gases your body produces are odorless, but a tiny percent are stinky sulfur-containing compounds that give farts their one-of-a-kind smell.

GEE WHIZ

The large intestine sends the water it absorbs into the bloodstream. But when your body has too *much* water, it

uses the water to flush out lots of other stuff it doesn't want. That's the kidneys' job.

Your *kidneys* are your body's janitors: they clean up the trash. Specifically, they filter all kinds of salts and waste chemicals out of your blood. It's a demanding schedule. They need to filter your body's entire blood supply every five minutes! Their job is so important that nature gave you a spare. If one of your kidneys has to be removed, the other one can get 50 percent bigger in just two months to compensate.

The kidneys send all these waste products, and any excess water you need to get rid of, into a stretchy holding tank called the *bladder*. Your bladder can get as big as a softball when it's full of urine.

The state of your urine can actually tell you quite a bit about you.

IF YOUR PEE IS . . .	Then you may . . .
unusually dark	need to drink more water
funny-smelling	have been eating asparagus
pinkish	have been eating beets (this is called beeturia)
sweet	have diabetes, and also why are you tasting your own pee?
in the pool	have bad swimming manners

EXTRA CREDIT

In ancient Egypt, women were the ones who urinated standing up, while men sat down! Did Cleopatra leave the seat up? The hieroglyphics are silent on this point.

AND IN THE END...

Once the large intestine has done its work, yesterday's food is stored in the rectum, ready to be expelled from the body. By now the food has been mixed with bile, giving it a brownish color. The undigested food will get

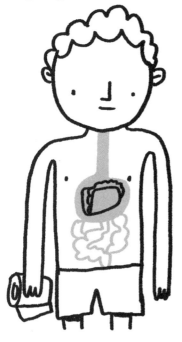

eliminated as *feces* the next time you poop.

And so our story ends right where we began: with the opening at the far end of our digestive tract. Normally the digestive highway is one that gets used only by food: burritos and pasta and so forth. But today we got to travel it as well. Thanks for coming along on this journey with me.

MUSIC CLASS

The body, of course, is what makes music possible. Without your fingers you could not play the piano. Without your knees you couldn't play the cello. Without

your nose you could not hum. (Go ahead, try it! Pinch your nose and hum. I bet you can't do it.)

But consider this: without the amazing human ear, there

would be no way to enjoy music at all!

Your ears aren't just the odd, flappy-looking handles on the sides of your head. Sure, those are important. The outer ear, or *pinna*, is specially shaped to gather sound waves. Your pinnae are . . .

STURDY! Indian strong-man Manjit Singh has used his ears to tow a seven-ton airplane.

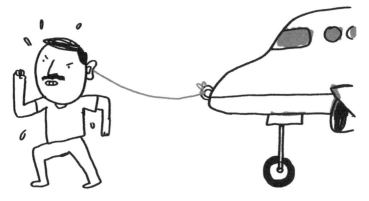

DECORATIVE! Earrings are much older than jewelry stores. Ötzi, a mummified five-thousand-year-old man pulled from an Alpine glacier in 1991, had pierced ears!

FLEXIBLE! About 15 percent of people can wiggle their ears. This is a leftover trait from our primate ancestors, who could aim their ears like satellite dishes to listen to things better.

But just like an iceberg, most of the ear is hidden beneath the surface.

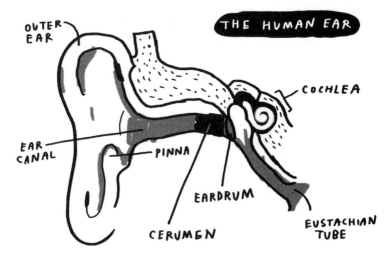

Sound waves collected by the outer ear are passed down the ear canal to the eardrum, causing the eardrum to vibrate. Your eardrum is a thin membrane so sensitive that if it moves *less than the width of a hydrogen atom*, your ear will detect sound!

Those vibrations get transferred via tiny bones up to the cochlea, which is a weird, snail-shaped thing filled with fluid. Tiny hairs get shaken up by the sound vibrations, creating nerve signals that get passed to the brain. *Ta-da!* Sound!

Of course, there are other vibrations in your ear, caused by muscles contracting and blood pumping and so on, but your brain is good at filtering those out so you don't hear them. Except if you somehow amplify that sound—then your brain will notice it. That's why people say that you can hear the ocean when you hold a seashell up to your ear. The rushing sound you hear is actually just the noises already around you.

Your ear canal is protected by some gunky stuff called *cerumen*—or, more commonly, "earwax." Early Saxons called the human pinkie the "ear finger," since it was so good for picking earwax. But I don't recommend using your finger to pick earwax. Even using Q-tips in your ears is a bad idea, since doing that can pack down the wax and lead to a lot of accidental injuries. (Punctured eardrums. Yuck.) Let the inside of your ear take care of its own cleaning, and you'll do much better.

And the number one

thing you can do to protect your ears? Keep them away from loudness! The music in your earphones can get louder than a lawn mower. A typical rock concert is as loud as a jet engine. So turn the volume down a little.

(A good rule of thumb is to listen to earphones at less than 60 percent volume for less than sixty minutes at a time.) That way your hearing will stay sharp and you can enjoy music for a life-

time! Or at least until you get old enough to think that all popular music has become terrible.

SIXTH PERIOD

PUMP IT UP

Earlier we talked about the strongest muscles in your body—the jaw, the calf, and so forth. But I left out the muscle that might be the toughest of all, one that has an around-the-clock job and never gets a single day of vacation or even a coffee break. It will flex more than 2.5 billion times over the course of your lifetime. I'm talking about your mouth, chatterbox. *No!* Just kidding. I'm talking about your heart.

MY HEART'S IN THE RIGHT PLACE

Pretend it's time for the national anthem or the Pledge of Allegiance or something, Junior Geniuses. Place your hand on your heart. *Wrong!*

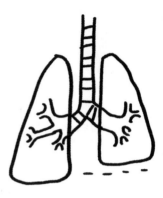

Most people assume that their heart is located on the left side of their body. It's actually right in the middle of your chest. But it may *feel* like it's beating on your left side, because the strongest part of the heart is on the left. Your left lung is actually a little smaller than the right, because of that slight tilt of your heart.

Unless you are the one person in every twelve thousand who has *dextrocardia*! In that case your heart is a pointed toward the right. It's not dangerous to have your heart tilt right instead of left, but it can sure confuse doctors for a minute!

CAN'T STOP, WON'T STOP

Ancient Greek philosophers such as Plato believed that the heart was the seat of emotions, especially anger. I'm glad Plato was a philosopher and not a surgeon. He also believed that the

liver was the organ of love and desire. If we believed him, valentine cards would be shaped like livers today.

The heart is *not* shaped much like a valentine, Junior Geniuses. It's a hollow muscle about the size of your fist, and it looks like this.

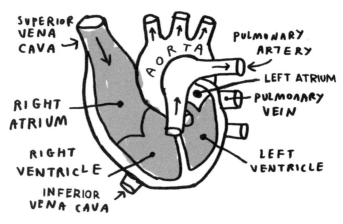

SUPERIOR VENA CAVA →

AORTA

PULMONARY ARTERY

LEFT ATRIUM

PULMONARY VEIN

RIGHT ATRIUM

RIGHT VENTRICLE

INFERIOR VENA CAVA ↗

LEFT VENTRICLE

The heart is there to work as a pump. When it squeezes, it pushes blood through your *circulatory system* of blood vessels. And that's quite a job, since your body has more than fifty thousand *miles* of blood vessels—long enough to circle the earth twice!

But the heart is up to the task. Each heartbeat is so powerful that it could squirt blood thirty feet! (If, you know, your heart were sitting on a table. Rather than in your chest. Where it belongs.) That force pushes blood all the way through your body and back three times every minute.

And the heart never gets tired, even though it needs to beat almost one million times *every week* just to keep you alive! Here's the amazing volume of blood your heart can pump:

To get that amount of liquid out of a kitchen faucet, you would have to leave it running uninterrupted for forty-five years straight!

(Also, it would be water, not blood. If blood comes out of your kitchen faucet for forty-five years straight, please contact your local utility company.)

EXTRA CREDIT

Your heart has its own electrical system, which means the heart will keep pumping even when removed from the human body! If it's placed in a liquid solution with the oxygen and ions it needs, a heart will keep beating on its own for more than half an hour.

ALL YOU NEED IS LUB

In 1816 a French doctor named René Laënnec needed to listen to a patient's heartbeat. But the patient was a pretty young woman, and Dr. Laënnec was too embar-

rassed to put his ear directly against her chest, which was the common medical practice of the time. Struck by a sudden inspiration, he rolled a piece of paper into a tube and placed one end to his ear and one end to her heart. He had just invented the first *stethoscope*!

When a doctor listens to your heart during an exam, he or she is hoping to hear this:

Lub-dub. Lub-dub. Lub-dub.

That's the sound of a healthy heart. Each sound is caused by valves closing between the chambers of your heart. The valves are little flaps of tissue that make sure blood flows in only one direction, like one-way doors at the supermarket.

The *lub* is the sound of valves closing at the top of your *ventricles*, so blood won't flow backward into your *atria* when the ventricles contract. The ventricles shoot blood out into your *arteries*. Then the *dub* is a different

set of valves closing: the ones between the ventricles and the arteries. Then the ventricles can relax and refill with new blood from the atria.

Sometimes the doctor hears other sounds in a heartbeat: a "slosh" or a "gallop" or a "murmur." Maybe a valve isn't closing all the way, or a ventricle is starting to fail. These sounds can help diagnose a problem before it turns fatal.

HOMEWORK

Tape a funnel into the end of an empty paper towel roll to make a simple home stethoscope. Listen to someone's heartbeat. Can you hear the *lub-dub*? Count how many times the heart beats in fifteen seconds and multiply by four. You've found your patient's resting heart rate! What do you think will happen to their heartbeat if you have them exercise for a minute and then you check again? Try it out.

THE BEAT GOT SICKER

Heart disease is still the leading cause of death for Americans, both men and women, and people of almost all races. But doctors today have some amazing tools in their medical bags when they need to tinker with your ticker.

Lifesaving balloons! When blood vessels get blocked and hardened, doctors do what's called a *balloon angioplasty*: They maneuver a tiny balloon through a patient's arteries to the right spot and blow it up. This widens the artery and improves blood flow. Then doctors can deflate the balloon and remove it.

Pork parts! When a heart valve malfunctions, today's doctors can replace it with one from an animal heart! Pig heart valves are very similar to ours, so "the other white meat" is the most popular choice.

Shock therapy! Electrical impulses make your heart beat regularly. If that stops working, doctors implant a tiny device called a *pacemaker* that shocks the heart every second or so, forcing it to *lub-dub* normally. Today's models are *much* better than the first pacemakers from the 1950s. Back then you had to plug yourself into a wall outlet if you wanted to regulate your heart rate!

Heart hoses! In 1929 a German doctor named Werner Forssmann believed he could save lives by inserting a small tube called a *catheter* into the human heart. But everyone else he talked to thought this would be fatal. Finally he proved he was right . . . by performing the operation on himself! He even tied a nurse to the operating table so that she would have to assist him. The risky operation was a success, and Forssmann later won the Nobel Prize.

Cyborg hearts! The first artificial heart design was patented in 1963 by the inventor Paul Winchell. (Winchell was also an actor and comedian—you probably know him best as the original voice of Winnie-the-Pooh's friend Tigger!) Today patients with heart failure can be implanted with mechanical devices called

VADs, or *ventricular assist devices*. Former vice president Dick Cheney has one, for example. Some VADs push blood through continuously, not with a series of *lub-dubs*. That's right, my friends: Dick Cheney has no pulse!

Of course, the best way to fix an unhealthy heart isn't a high-tech gadget. It's a healthy lifestyle! As a grown-up you'll be able to reduce your risk of heart disease by a whopping 85 percent just by eating well, exercising regularly, and not smoking.

EXTRA CREDIT

The most popular day of the year to have a heart attack? According to emergency room doctors, it's December 25, followed by December 26. This is due to a combination of cold temperatures, holiday stress, and all the big-time eating and drinking that goes on at this time of year.

ALL ABOARD!

Maybe the best way to see how blood flows through your heart and lungs is with a picture. Have you ever seen a map of a train or subway system? Your circulatory system is a kind of mass transit system, but instead of commuters, it delivers things such as oxygen, nutrients, and hormones.

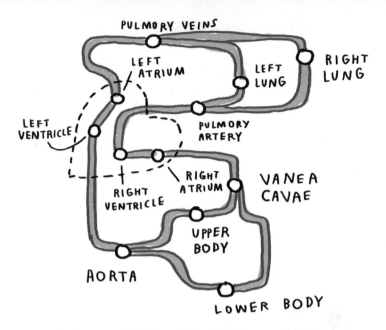

The heart is the Grand Central Terminal of this train line. Blood comes from being oxygenated in the lungs and flows through the *pulmonary veins* into the *left atrium* of the heart. Then the blood gets squeezed from the left atrium into the *left ventricle*, and then leaves the heart via the *aorta*, your body's biggest artery. After circulating little oxygen passengers through your whole body, the blood train returns to the heart via the *venae cavae*, your body's biggest veins. (Arteries carry blood away from the heart, and veins bring it back.) At this point the train is mostly empty—it's out of oxygen. The blood flows through the venae cavae into the *right atrium*, and then into the *right ventricle*. From the right ventricle the *pulmonary artery* carries blood to the lungs for a new load of oxygen, and the cycle begins again.

From the arteries and to the veins, blood travels through all the tissues of your body via teeny, tiny little vessels called *capillaries*. The smallest capillaries are four times as narrow as a human hair. Veins and arteries, on the other hand, can get very big. The femoral arteries that carry blood to your legs are as big as your finger. The aorta can grow as thick as a garden hose!

AIR AND ERROR

The ancient Greek physician Hippocrates is called the "father of Western medicine." In fact, to this day new doctors still take an oath named for him. But Hippocrates didn't know everything about medicine. For example, he decided that arteries carried air around the body! Everyone believed this for the next four hundred years, until the Greek doctor Galen realized that the circulatory system was actually for blood, not air.

The ancients also believed—wrongly—that the fourth finger was the only part of the hand connected directly by a vein to the heart. Today that's why people traditionally wear wedding rings on that finger!

Sometimes we get the idea that oxygenated blood is red and deoxygenated blood is blue. It's true that your veins *look* blue under your skin, but that's just an illusion. Blood in your veins is still red, though it's a duller shade of red once its oxygen is gone. Call it maroon, maybe. But when those maroon veins are seen through skin, they look bluish.

You know that numb "pins and needles" feeling you get when part of your body "falls asleep"? That's related to the arteries as well. When too much pressure is put on a limb, the blood vessels get squished and blood supply is cut off from the nerves. Then the nerves get compressed as well, cutting off communication between your limb and your brain. The tingling as your foot "wakes up" is caused by scrambled nerves getting a boost of oxygen from a sudden flow of blood.

WINDBAGS

Like your heart, your lungs can never rest, because your cells can't function without oxygen. Not for long, anyway—although in 2012 a German diver set a new world record for holding his breath underwater. He went twenty-two minutes and twenty-two seconds between breaths!

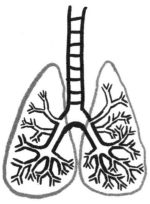

When you inhale, air travels down your windpipe into two tubes called the *bronchi*.

The bronchi split in two.

Then each branch splits in two again.

This happens many, many more times!

By this time the air tubes are very small indeed. Each of these half billion tiny passageways ends in a little balloon, which is called an *alveolus*. The alveoli transfer oxygen from the air of each breath into your lungs' fifteen hundred *miles* of capillaries.

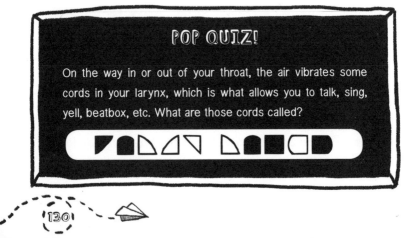

POP QUIZ!

On the way in or out of your throat, the air vibrates some cords in your larynx, which is what allows you to talk, sing, yell, beatbox, etc. What are those cords called?

Every day you breathe more than thirty-five pounds of air. (If you add those pounds up over the course of your lifetime, that air would weigh as much as a 747 airplane!) And each breath contains a *lot* of air molecules—20,000,000,000,000,000,000,000 molecules, to be precise. When you breathe out, those air molecules (oxygen, nitrogen, carbon dioxide, and so on) get mixed back into the atmosphere, until someone breathes them in again.

You know what that means, Junior Geniuses? Take a breath and hold it. There is air in your lungs right now that was breathed by a dinosaur. In fact, there's a 98.2 percent chance that you have an air molecule in your lungs right now that Julius Caesar exhaled *in his very last breath* when he died in 44 BC! The same goes for the last breath of Michelangelo or Abraham Lincoln or anyone else in history. Do you detect a whiff of peanut butter and banana sandwiches? That must be a molecule from Elvis's last breath.

Whoa. Okay, you can breathe out now.

THIS BLOOD'S FOR YOU

If you are not interested in blood, Junior Geniuses, you are really missing out. Of course, if you are a little *too* interested in blood, you might be a vampire. Hopefully we can find a good level of interest right in the middle.

Blood makes up 8 percent of your body weight—about five quarts in a grown-up. That's enough to supply 1.2 million mosquito bites! But you don't want all your blood going to bugs. You need it for dozens of things—not just to circulate oxygen but also to get vitamins and sugars around your body, to collect waste products, to warm some parts of your body and cool others, to fight infection. . . . Blood does it all!

When you are old enough (usually sixteen or seventeen), I highly recommend that you donate blood—not

to mosquitoes but to the Red Cross. Every two seconds someone in the United States needs a transfusion, and there's no artificial substitute for real human blood. So you could literally be saving a life every time you donate! Over the course of a lifetime, you could donate 46.5 gallons of sweet, sweet life-giving blood.

When blood is drawn out of your arm into a test tube, it looks like this.

But then the Red Cross will spin the blood in a *centrifuge*. ("Centrifuge" is Latin for "spinny machine thing.") Surprise! Now it looks like this:

The spinning has pushed the dense parts of your blood to the bottom, and left the lightest parts on top. We can clearly see three layers. Turn the page to see them, from top to bottom.

Plasma. The liquid part of your blood—not just water, but also proteins, sugar, hormones, and a bunch of other stuff. Want to see what plasma looks like without giving blood? Pop a blister. The liquid inside a blister is more or less plasma.

White blood cells. The body's soldiers—they patrol the blood, looking for infections, and when they find one, they gang up on it.

Platelets. Their job is to "clot" your blood when it leaks. That's why a scab forms when you get hurt. Without that scab, you'd just keep bleeding until you were out of blood.

Red blood cells. They deliver oxygen to your cells, using a protein called *hemoglobin* that's good at binding to oxygen. The secret ingredient in hemoglobin is actually iron. You have enough iron in your blood to make one three-inch nail!

I FEEL THE NEED! THE NEED . . . TO BLEED!

When your body is sick, that's when you really need your red and white blood cells the most. But until about 150 years ago, doctors didn't know that. They treated lots of illnesses with something called *bloodletting*—intentionally draining blood from their patients! Sometimes they even used leeches, gross bloodsucking water worms! Millions of patients were harmed or killed by bloodletting over the years—including George Washington.

THE SCARLET LETTERS

Doctors performing blood transfusions have to be careful, because not all blood is the same. There are different proteins called *antigens* in different people's blood, and if you get an injection of the wrong antigens, it can be fatal. There are four common blood types: A, B, AB, and O.

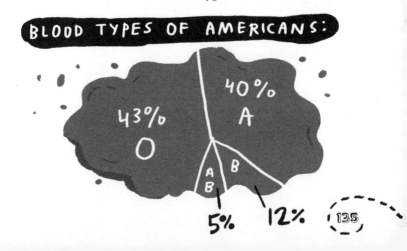

BLOOD TYPES OF AMERICANS:

43% O

40% A

AB 5%

B 12%

EXTRA CREDIT

There's also an extremely rare blood antigen type called *Bombay blood*. In most of the world it's found in only one person in every million. In Mumbai, India (the city formerly called Bombay), it's much more common.

AB blood is called the *universal recipient*, because people with AB blood can accept transfusions from any other blood type safely. O, on the other hand, is the universal donor. Everyone can accept O-type blood safely.

In Japan it's believed that blood type is an accurate way to measure personality and compatibility, sort of the way we use astrology. Instead of "What's your sign? I bet you're a Gemini!" a Japanese person might say, "What's your type? I bet you're AB!"

But even if you have no plans to hit the Tokyo singles scene anytime soon, it's important to learn your blood type, my friends. That way doctors will know how to treat you in an emergency!

SEVENTH PERIOD

IN SICKNESS AND IN HEALTH

As you have probably heard many times from nagging grown-ups, life can be dangerous. The World Health Organization lists 12,420 different categories of diseases in its official list. And that doesn't even include problems like "a bad case of the Mondays."

Luckily, we're not defenseless against disease. Our bodies are on the case.

THE WAR ON BUGS

I've already told you that white blood cells are the body's army against infection. What I didn't tell you is that, just like an army, it has a whole bunch of weapons at its disposal. Let's meet the troops.

Neutrophils. These cells are the blood's kamikaze pilots. They swarm at the first sign of an attack and bravely sacrifice their own lives in the defense. Have you ever seen a wound with that white gunky stuff called *pus*? Pus is made of millions of dead neutrophils.

Eosinophils and basophils. These are "Special Forces" cells that the body deploys to fight parasitic infections, like worms and ticks.

Monocytes. These spies can actually leave the bloodstream and infiltrate tissues and organs. They can also grow into . . .

Macrophages. These white blood cells are the tanks of the immune system. They mow down all enemies in their path, absorbing them like a vacuum cleaner would.

NK cells. The *NK* is for "natural killer," so these guys have the scariest name of any blood cell. Like snipers, they can tell infected cells from healthy ones and take out very specific targets.

Helper T cells. These are the "generals" of the blood army, calling vast troops of white blood cells (called *T* and *B cells*) to action.

The great thing about T and B cells is that once they've neutralized an enemy, they remember how they killed it. The next time they meet that type of bacteria, it won't stand a chance.

In fact, that's how vaccinations work. Nobody likes getting shots, but you should *thank* your doctors when they jab you in the arm with that big, sharp needle. (Don't you hate it when they call it a "little pinch" or a "poke"? Liars.) These shots mimic dangerous diseases but usually don't cause any symptoms. So they're like target practice for your white blood cells. If the real disease ever shows up, your body is now ready and waiting for it. This is called *immunity*.

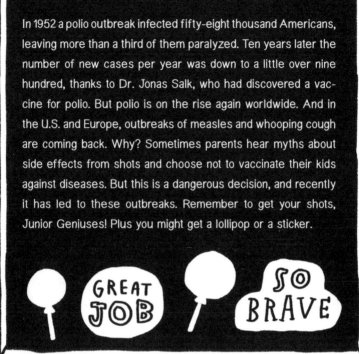

EXTRA CREDIT

In 1952 a polio outbreak infected fifty-eight thousand Americans, leaving more than a third of them paralyzed. Ten years later the number of new cases per year was down to a little over nine hundred, thanks to Dr. Jonas Salk, who had discovered a vaccine for polio. But polio is on the rise again worldwide. And in the U.S. and Europe, outbreaks of measles and whooping cough are coming back. Why? Sometimes parents hear myths about side effects from shots and choose not to vaccinate their kids against diseases. But this is a dangerous decision, and recently it has led to these outbreaks. Remember to get your shots, Junior Geniuses! Plus you might get a lollipop or a sticker.

GREAT JOB

SO BRAVE

YOUR OWN WORST ENEMY

Immune responses explain a lot of things that happen to you when you get sick. These symptoms can be annoying, but your body is actually trying to help you out.

Let's say you have the flu. "Flu" is short for "influenza," meaning "influence." In medieval times people thought epidemics were caused by the influence of the stars.

Headache. A sign that your body is releasing chemical messengers called *cytokines*.

Fever. Your body has warmed up in hopes of killing off bacteria, which can be very picky about temperature.

Runny nose. You are making more mucus to flush out germs.

Swollen glands. Little factories called *lymph nodes* are producing millions of new soldier cells to join the fight.

GESUNDHEIT!

Warning! Sometimes these defense systems can go haywire. On January 13, 1981, a British girl named Donna Griffiths suddenly began sneezing uncontrollably. She continued to sneeze at least once every few minutes *for the next three years*!

Just like with a real army, when the immune system gets out of control, the results can be serious. In some cases the body even mistakes its own tissues for the disease and starts attacking itself! These *autoimmune* diseases include:

lupus

multiple sclerosis

type 1 diabetes

celiac disease

rheumatoid arthritis

psoriasis

Autoimmune diseases are hard to diagnose and, so far, impossible to cure. With most diseases there's a "bug" to attack—a virus or bacteria. But with autoimmune diseases the bug is the patient! The best doctors can do is manage the symptoms.

EXTRA CREDIT

Friedrich Bischinger, an Austrian doctor, recommends a novel way to build up your immunity—by eating your boogers! "People who pick their nose and eat it get a natural boost to their immune system for free," he says. But not until after class, please. I don't need to see that.

COLD WAR

Wait a minute! If our bodies remember how to fight sickness every time we beat one, why do we keep getting colds every winter of our lives? Shouldn't our first cold also be our last?

The problem is that the "common cold" is actually caused by more than two hundred *different* viruses. And they're always changing slightly, which makes them a moving target for your body—or any scientist trying to discover a cold vaccine.

Mom and Dad may have been right all along when it comes to preventing and treating colds. A 2005 study in Wales found that subjects were more likely to catch colds when their feet were cold and wet, so bundling up in the winter might not be a bad idea. And a 2000 study in

Nebraska found that one of the best liquids for relieving cold symptoms was . . . chicken soup!

Even if the future doesn't bring a cure for the cold, *your* future will bring fewer colds—because kids catch more colds than adults. Kindergartners average six to eight colds every year, but adults get only two or three. At any age the best way to treat a cold or flu is not to catch it in the first place. Regular hand-washing, especially during cold season, is the way to go. Doctors say more hand-washing with soap could save more than a million lives every year!

HOMEWORK

When you wash your hands, sing the alphabet song all the way through before you finish! That way you'll be sure to scrub for the full doctor-recommended twenty seconds.

GLOBAL HEALTH

Unless you travel the world as tirelessly as I do, Junior Geniuses, here are some unusual diseases you are unlikely to see. (Or catch.)

PAPUA NEW GUINEA

KURU. The Fore tribe calls it "the laughing sickness," because it leads to uncontrollable shaking and giggling before it kills you. We now know that kuru is transmitted through cannibalism. The Fore people ate one another's brains! Kuru is actually related to mad cow disease—but with human meat instead of beef.

JUMPING FRENCHMEN OF MAINE.

NORTHERN MAINE

In the late nineteenth century, fifty French Canadian lumberjacks were diagnosed with an odd disorder: They would jump wildly in the air and freak out whenever startled by the tiniest things. While like this, they would sometimes repeat every sound that they heard, and even obey random commands.

NODDING SYNDROME.

SOUTH SUDAN, UGANDA, and TANZANIA

Is it caused by a parasite? A vitamin deficiency? Chemical weapons? Nobody knows why some children in East Africa get this strange disease that stops their growth and causes nodding seizures whenever they see food.

HYPERTRICHOSIS.

MEXICO

In the Aceves family of Zacatecas, Mexico, twenty-four people have this incredibly rare genetic condition. It's been called *werewolf syndrome* because it causes hair to grow all over the face and body.

PARIS SYNDROME. Every year about one dozen Japanese tourists in Paris get overwhelmed by the City of Light and report hallucinations, dizziness, and a heart rate racing out of control. Psychiatrists think Paris syndrome may have to do with culture and language barriers, or the way that Paris is portrayed in the Japanese media.

But there's one disease you won't find anywhere on the map: smallpox! Smallpox probably killed about half a billion people in the history of the world, but in 1796 a doctor named Edward Jenner noticed that British milkmaids never seemed to catch it. He wondered if a disease called *cowpox* might have been making these dairy

workers immune to smallpox. He was right! Cowpox became the very first vaccination—in fact, the word "vaccination" comes from "*vacca*," Latin for "cow."

The vaccination worked. In 1977 a hospital cook in Somalia was diagnosed with the very last case of naturally occurring smallpox ever. Today the only samples are found in heavily guarded laboratories. It's the first disease ever completely eradicated by humankind.

NEATNESS COUNTS

There's a surprising health threat that still causes seven thousand deaths and 1.5 million injuries in this country every year—bad handwriting! This may sound like a joke, but those numbers are real! Doctors are famous for their messy writing, which can lead to trouble when prescriptions are filled. Tell your doctor to write neatly, Junior Geniuses! Otherwise, you might not know if you have *inscrutable* or *charming*!

THE CUTTING EDGE

A century before Edward Jenner, British medicine wasn't so amazing. When King Charles II was dying in 1685, his doctors tried everything to save him. They shaved his head and burned his scalp with hot irons, drained his blood, covered his feet in pigeon poop, and fed him "extract of human skull." After five days of this, Charles apologized to his court for taking so long to die . . . and soon died.

Medicine has come a long way since the seventeenth century. Today you wouldn't believe some of the things doctors can do:

◦ Perform full face and hand transplants!

◦ Put paralyzed people in brain-controlled exoskeletons that let them walk and even play soccer!

◦ Grow new skin to treat burn patients. It takes just a week to grow a whole basketball court's worth of skin!

◦ Detect cancer just by having specially trained dogs sniff patients' breath!

MEDICAL MYSTERY TOUR

In your lifetime I'm sure you'll see medical advances that make those look like pigeon poop. But it's strange how much about our bodies we still don't understand.

Doctors aren't even sure what causes lots of everyday health problems:

GROWING PAINS ? STUTTERING ?
HICCUPS ? { ASTHMA } ' CANKER SORES
? ? ?
BIRTHMARKS ? BABY ?
? ?? ? COLIC ?

"Growing pains" actually have nothing to do with growing! Half of all kids get these occasional aches in the muscles of their arms and legs. Doctors have no idea what cause them, but these pains don't seem to correspond with growth spurts. (Also, limb growth takes place at joints, not in your muscles.)

Maybe someday *you* will be the Junior Genius who solves one of these medical mysteries.

WELL, WELL, WELL

Of course, good health isn't just a matter of not being sick. If you have the flu, you feel terrible. If you don't have the flu but you eat a bag of jelly beans instead of breakfast, guess what? *You will also feel terrible!*

Since you can't always control when you get sick, making healthy choices is the best way to feel good! Please copy this handy chart onto a leaf of healthy organic kale and carry it around with you at all times:

DON'T . . .

Live on a strict diet of jelly sandwiches on white bread with potato chips.

Drink sugary sodas and fruit drinks.

Play video games until your eyes bleed and you accidentally call your dad "Mario."

Stay up all night reading Junior Genius Guides with a flashlight.

Drink or smoke or do drugs.

DO . . .

Eat lots of fruit, vegetables, and whole grains.

Drink plenty of water and low-fat milk.

Get an hour of exercise a day. Run around. Jump up and down. Yell.

Get about nine hours of sleep—or whatever amount makes you feel rested, not crabby.

Think and joke and chew bugs.

Being healthy doesn't mean that you can *never* eat fast food or drink a giant soda or lie around watching TV all day. It just means those should not become habits. I want you all to live long and healthy lives, so you can take care of me in my old age.

On second thought, don't chew bugs. I changed my mind about that one.

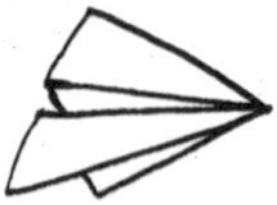

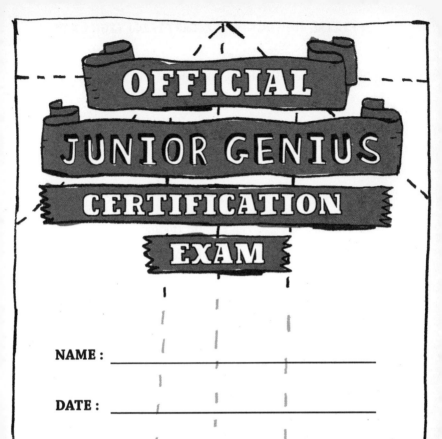

OFFICIAL
JUNIOR GENIUS
CERTIFICATION
EXAM

NAME : _____

DATE : _____

In this guide we've learned about the human body from head to toe. But how much of that information do you currently have stored from ear to ear? (HINT: that's where your brain is.) Get a number 2 pencil in your dominant hand and turn the page when I tell you to begin.

Wait for it.

Wait for it. . . .

BEGIN.

1. Where would you find the hardest substance in your body?

    Ⓐ Your teeth   Ⓑ Your heart

    Ⓒ Your bones   Ⓓ Your joints

2. A substance called melanin determines what about your hair?

    Ⓐ Curliness   Ⓑ Thickness

    Ⓒ Color   Ⓓ Length

3. What molecule in your body contains your entire biological instructions?

    Ⓐ Carbon   Ⓑ Cholesterol

    Ⓒ DNA   Ⓓ Hemoglobin

4. Which disease was completely eradicated by scientists by the late 1970s?

    Ⓐ Smallpox   Ⓑ Influenza

    Ⓒ Polio   Ⓓ Lupus

5. What happens in the space inside your bones?

    Ⓐ Water is absorbed   Ⓑ Ligaments attach

    Ⓒ Bile is stored   Ⓓ Blood cells are made

6. What is your body's biggest organ?

Ⓐ The brain   Ⓑ The skin

Ⓒ The stomach   Ⓓ The tongue

7. Fill in the blank. The difference between veins and arteries is that the veins _____?

Ⓐ Are smaller   Ⓑ Return to the heart

Ⓒ Carry oxygenated blood   Ⓓ Have valves

8. The cerebellum, hippocampus, and thalamus are all parts of what?

Ⓐ The lung   Ⓑ The brain

Ⓒ The digestive system   Ⓓ A cell

9. What's the leading cause of death in America today?

Ⓐ Cancer   Ⓑ Diabetes

Ⓒ Car accidents   Ⓓ Heart disease

10. What do you do when the muscle called the diaphragm suddenly spasms?

Ⓐ Hiccup   Ⓑ Yawn

Ⓒ Sneeze   Ⓓ Swallow

11. Which of your senses works because of vibrations in your cochlea?

(A) Sight   (B) Hearing

(C) Smell   (D) Taste

12. What part of the digestive system absorbs most of the nutrients from your food?

(A) The mouth   (B) The stomach

(C) The small intestine   (D) The colon

13. A, B, AB, and O are the four major types of what?

(A) DNA bases   (B) Blood

(C) Nerves   (D) Viruses

14. What change happens in your eyes when you step into a dark room?

(A) Your retinas move forward (B) Your corneas flatten

(C) Your pupils expand   (D) Your irises dim

15. Which type of muscle works without your having to consciously control it?

(A) Skeletal   (B) Fast-twitch

(C) Slow-twitch   (D) Smooth

16. Nerve impulses carry signals across tiny little gaps called what?

Ⓐ Synapses   Ⓑ Ribosomes

Ⓒ Capillaries   Ⓓ Fontanelles

17. Which type of blood cell fights infection for you?

Ⓐ Platelets   Ⓑ Red blood cells

Ⓒ White blood cells   Ⓓ Plasma

18. Where would you find one-quarter of all the bones in your body?

Ⓐ Your skull   Ⓑ Your ribs

Ⓒ Your spinal column   Ⓓ Your two feet

19. What is unusual about the drugs called placebos?

Ⓐ They suppress the immune system   Ⓑ They are addictive

Ⓒ They are vaccinations   Ⓓ They contain no medicine

20. What does your stomach use to break down food?

Ⓐ Hydrochloric acid   Ⓑ Insulin

Ⓒ Bilirubin   Ⓓ Cytokines

All right, pencils down! Turn the page to the
answers and see how you did.

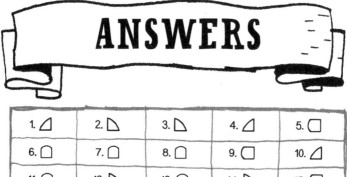

ANSWERS

1. △	2. ◺	3. ◺	4. △	5. ◻
6. ◻	7. ◻	8. ◻	9. ◻	10. △
11. ◻	12. ◺	13. ◻	14. ◺	15. ◻
16. △	17. ◺	18. ◻	19. ◻	20. △

SCORING

16—20	Certified Junior Genius!
13—15	Missed by a Hair
10—12	Showed a Lot of Heart
6—9	Took It on the Chin
0—5	Did Not De-Liver

Did you pass? Nicely done! You should definitely print out an official certificate at JuniorGeniusGuides.com and display it proudly.

But if not, I don't want to see any lacrimal secretions! (Also known as tears.) When you were a baby, your brain was creating two million new synapses *every second*! To pass this exam you just need to make twenty more. Review what we've learned in this guide, and try the test again. You too will be a Junior Genius before long!

HOMEWORK

We learned a lot in this guide, Junior Geniuses, but our bodies do so many amazing things that we didn't have time to look at. We only got the "bare bones," if you'll forgive the expression. If you want to bulk up your anatomy knowledge with more fun projects, here are a few ideas I just had.

○ **SLEEP IN A GIANT EYE.** Do you know what a *camera obscura* is? Basically you can turn your whole bedroom into a giant eyeball, and old-timey science and art people used to do it for fun. You'll need to completely block your windows with posterboard or something, but leave a hole (or "pupil"!) for a lens bor-rowed from a flashlight. When the light is right, and if the room is dark enough, the outside view will be projected onto the oppo-site wall, just like on a retina. The view will even be upside down!

○ **STRAIN YOUR BRAIN.** Do you think long words are the hardest to remember? Short words can be just as tricky. There are ten parts of your body that have only three letters. (Slang terms don't count, so there's no "gut," "lap," or "bum.") I guarantee there will be smoke coming out of your eyes by the time you think of all ten.

○ **GET PHYSICAL.** Your body does so much for you. Do you know if you're giving it the hour of exercise that it needs every day? For two weeks try keeping a log of how

much time you spend on different exercises: playing outside, going for a walk, sports. Also, add a daily set of one simple exercise that you like (jumping jacks, maybe, or modified push-ups) and mark in your log how many you could do before you got too tired. If that number starts going up, you're getting in better shape!

○ **DESIGN A NEW PAIR OF GENES.** We talked a little bit about heredity in this guide, but we didn't really get the chance to play with how it works. Choose two of your favorite fictional characters and draw what you think their offspring would look like. Are SpongeBob SquarePants and Miss Piggy expecting a baby? What about Bugs Bunny and Dora the Explorer? Every time you have to make a genetic decision (eye color, head

shape, number of limbs, etc.), flip a coin to see which parent's trait the kid will be blessed with. I predict some odd-looking babies—but believe me, that can happen in real life as well.

THE FINAL BELL

Did you know that in ancient Egypt . . .

∘ People worshipped a god of lettuce?

∘ Everyone shaved their eyebrows when a cat died?

∘ It took thirty thousand workers to build one funeral monument?

Is your brain full of information yet? I hope you have a little room left, because I'll be back soon with **Ken Jennings' Junior Genius Guides: Ancient Egypt.** Fasten your seat belts, because it's going to be a wild, wild ride. OF LEARNING!

Life is always more fun when you're learning stuff, so until we meet again, let's all keep in our hearts the official Junior Genius slogan, which I stole from a great philosopher named Blaise Pascal (1623–1662).

"It is much better to know something about everything than everything about something."

Class dismissed!

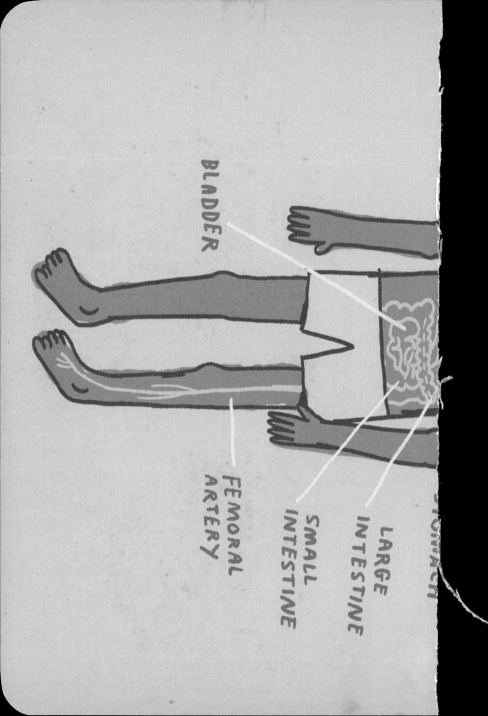